THE MARTIN LUTHER KING, JR., PLAGIARISM STORY

Edited by Theodore Pappas

The Rockford Institute
Rockford, Illinois

Library of Congress
Catalog Card Number

Pappas, Theodore
1994   93-085405

ISBN 0-9619364-5-2

For Daniel, Jean, Tracey, and Melissa

CONTENTS

*I am against the prophets, saith the Lord, that
steal my words every one from his neighbour.*
—Jeremiah 23:30

*. . . an inferior genius may, without any
imputation of servility, pursue the path of the
ancients, provided he declines to tread in
their footsteps.*
—Samuel Johnson,
The Rambler, No. 143

*Plagiarize,
Let no one else's work evade your eyes,
Remember why the good Lord made your eyes,
So don't shade your eyes,
But plagiarize, plagiarize, plagiarize—
Only be sure always to call it please "research."*
—Tom Lehrer, "Lobachevsky"

ACKNOWLEDGMENTS

"Some books are written for the pleasure or the zest of it. Other books are written as a painful duty, because there is something that needs to be said—and because other people have better sense than to say it." Thomas Sowell's introductory remarks to his 1984 book *Civil Rights: Rhetoric or Reality?* aptly describe the volume that follows. There could be no more thankless enterprise or reckless pursuit, no endeavor more potentially destructive of personal and professional ties, than a sustained critical study of such a hallowed figure as Martin Luther King, Jr. The foolishness of such a venture is doubtless obvious by the host of nationally influential editors and publishers who knew about this story as well as of its veracity but who nevertheless suppressed it and continue to whitewash it today.

According to Pulitzer Prize-winning biographer David Garrow (in the June 1991 *Journal of American History*) and King Papers editor Clayborne Carson of Stanford University (in *Palimpsest: Editorial Theory in the Humanities*, University of Michigan Press, 1993), I am King's harshest critic on this matter of plagiarism. I acknowledge this with neither pride nor perniciousness, but merely to place in proper perspective the work that follows and the enormous debt this project owes to a number of courageous individuals still devoted to what T.S. Eliot called "the permanent things." Special thanks are due to Thomas Fleming, the editor of *Chronicles*; the board of directors of The Rockford Institute, which consented to publish this book; and Allan Carlson, the publisher of *Chronicles* and president of The Rockford Institute. Without their unfailing support and stubborn commitment to principle over politics, this story would never have been covered by *Chronicles* in the first place, let alone exposed in its entirety over the last four years.

I wish also to thank Jacob Neusner, for writing the foreword—a stauncher defender of academic integrity could never be found; historian John Lukacs and nationally syndicated columnist Samuel Francis, for their constructive criticisms and kind words of support; Michael Warder, executive vice president of The Rockford Institute, for helping to spread the word about this story and book; Leann Dobbs and Christine Haynes, for their editorial assistance with the manuscript; Anna Mycek-Wodecki, for the graphic cover; and Anita Fedora, Amanda Lundgren, Joyce Howell, and Guy Reffett, for their extensive help with production of the book. Lastly I wish to thank my wife Melissa, who has graciously persevered more ranting about plagiarism and parallel quotations than anyone should have to tolerate in a lifetime. Her patience and indulgence have not been unappreciated.

T.P.
Rockford, Illinois
January 1994

FOREWORD

This collection of documents records how the academic world confronted the fact that a revered American was a plagiarist. The Reverend Martin Luther King, Jr.'s place in history is secure by reason of his memorable leadership of the civil rights movement. But those who have transformed him into an icon to be polished, instead of accepting him as a great man whose great deeds are to be emulated but whose considerable flaws are to be noted and avoided, want more. They define the politically correct judgment of King's life in terms that defy plausibility, that deny the man that humanity which rendered all the more sublime the achievements of his mature intellect; his public advocacy of nonviolence; his insistence—sorely missed today—that a single law govern white and black, Jew and gentile, man and woman; above all, his courageous leadership of black Americans in a time of crisis.

From the point at which Mr. Pappas laid out the evidence that King stole a fair part of his doctoral dissertation and other writings, the engines of political correctness raised steam and sounded their whistles. The mere fact that this book could find no publisher other than Mr. Pappas's own sponsor makes one wonder what need we have for guarantees of freedom of the press—let alone free speech. The press, after all, rarely accords a cordial welcome to those who violate its rigid norms of what may and may not be thought, therefore said. But if the press and world of publishing may find little in which to take pride in their response to the embarrassing facts turned up in these pages, what is to be said of the academy?

The answer is found in the pages of this book, and it does not offer much reassurance to those who hope that this country's universities may meet their responsibility to truth, integrity, and national renewal. The press and the publishing world, which exist to make money, have fared no better: publishers want to sell more than one book, and publishing this one—so they feared—would mark them for a long, dismal future. But the press and the book publishers claim no moral authority; everyone knows who they are and what they do. By contrast, the professors, provosts, deans, and presidents addressed in these pages all represent themselves as scholars; they have taken learning as their vocation and so profess to care for what is true and can be shown to be true; and, we must not forget, all of them also enjoy lifetime tenure in their academic positions, if not in their administrative ones.

So society accords them security and privilege, hoping in exchange to gain the benefit of objective criticism and sustained truthtelling. Then, while elements of the press can always be found to form the exception to the rule of cowardice, on the one side, and rigid conformity, on the other, what excuse can we find to explain the conduct, in the present controversy, of those who, impregnable in tenure, endowed with the prestige accruing to the academy, protected from reprisal by law and custom, turned their back on the facts? Or, worse still, what are we to make of those who explain away and justify in terms of the peculiar culture of black Americans actions that, when done by other Americans, are penalized? Demeaning to blacks and a self-serving cover for deep racism, the excuses for King's thefts—that is, his using without attribution enormous tracts of writing not his own—bear a brutal judgment. Only the academy as we know it in these troubled times can issue racist judgments in the name of intellect, inventing for the occasion categories and classifications to stigmatize entire races as subject to a moral law different from that ordinary folk obey.

And that meretricious, condescending defense of King's thievery is precisely what people offered when Pappas asked his tough, embarrassing questions. They lied, they told half-truths, they made up fables, they did everything they could but address facts. In the face of their own university's rules against plagiarism, Boston University's academic authorities and professors somehow found excuses for King's plagiarism. They found extenuating circumstances, they reworded matters to make them sound less dreadful, they compromised their own university's integrity and the rules supposedly enforced to defend and protect the processes of learning and the consequent degrees. They called into question the very standing of the university as a place where cheating is penalized and misrepresentation condemned. And all this, why? I suspect it stems from insufficient faith in the authentic achievements of Martin Luther

King, Jr., a greater concern to explain away the flaws of his life's record than to set them in the balance against the glories of his brief, courageous life.

Why, we therefore have to ask ourselves, must Martin Luther King be remembered in an implausible image of perfection, when the full and human man leaves a so much greater heritage of human achievement: courage, perseverance, insistence upon the equality of every American before the law, uncompromising demand for justice for each of us? That did not suffice, and instead a systematic campaign to discredit irrefutable facts aimed at giving the country a Martin Luther King whom everyone must confront not as a great man but only as a perfect God. But (in the language of Christianity, which King spoke) only One was God Incarnate, and only One has risen from the dead. Was not King all the greater for the natural man he transcended in his quest for justice for all Americans? Is not the civil rights movement of the 1960's, which did tear down the old American structure of legal racism, a monument to King's capacity for moral leadership of all Americans? Did this man not die—knowingly give up his life in a dangerous venture—for the things he espoused?

Yes, King was all the greater, the movement does serve as his monument, and the man knew precisely the risks he took and the price he would pay. What more can a man achieve with scarcely four decades on this earth than King achieved for blacks among all Americans? What more do his latter-day apologists want for him? What Pappas brings into question is not King's greatness, but the divinity that has descended about him and isolated and alienated him from the realm of the human, which he in his life graced more than disgraced—much more.

Pappas's observations about Coleridge and King—"both men plagiarized some of their most influential prose and were publicly exposed as pilferers only after death"—bring to mind the critical question for the academy. What was at stake in trying to suppress what in the end would inexorably rise to the surface? Rumor has it that King's doctoral committee recognized the problem of plagiarism and instructed him to provide the documentation that the academy's ethics required. The dissertation was filed and accepted without the corrections and revisions being made; no one followed up. That rumor evidently means to mitigate the stark and awful truth that Boston University bestowed an earned doctorate for work that did not meet the accepted standards of honesty and scholarship.

If the story is so, then King presumably deposited whatever was in hand; no one checked. But in universities, we are supposed to check; that is what we are paid to do. Society assigns us the task of intellectual integrity: someone out there has to say how things are, without bias or cunning. That is why King was not well-served; the faculty owed him their careful criticism not only of his ideas and mode of setting them forth, demonstrating them, addressing possible objections to them, but also of his presentation of those ideas in written form, including the usual references to what he had consulted—all the more, what he had quoted. The awful suspicion lurks that a lower standard applied to blacks than whites, and it is difficult to suppress the question of whether the professors at Boston University might have imputed to their black students lesser capacities than those they saw in whites.

In the past few years Pappas has found little grounds for confidence in the academy's integrity. Corrupted by its own peculiar brand of tolerance, the academy tergiversated. Ignoble synonyms may also serve: apostatize, desert, rat, renounce, repudiate, dodge, evade, hedge, pussyfoot, shuffle, sidestep, and weasel. Jon Westling's letter to *Chronicles* set the record straight—but as the reader will see, it was straight to hell, not exactly the direction the acting president of Boston University had in mind. What he showed was his university's policy, which was concede nothing, especially not the facts. That makes all the more stark the side-by-side citations of King's and Jack Boozer's writings. The comparison opens the question of whether, without Boozer, King had a dissertation at all. One need not follow Pappas's righteous—and understandable—indignation to its end. I wish he had not contemplated the phrase "strip King of his degree." Posthumous acts of that kind strike me as vengeful, but also vacuous, no less than posthumous honors, for that matter. But, in the context of the moment in which he wrote that essay, addressing people who in defending an icon undertook to fabricate a massive tissue of lies, who can fail to grasp the provocation?

Charles Babington tells the story of the publishers and editors who suppressed the facts. But he does not list the writers and scholars—"several historians"—who declined to write the story. Martin Peretz of the *New Republic* explained that the story had "racial overtones." But acts of omission mattered more. It is what people did not say, would not do, declined to publish, refused to investigate, that shows us the true character of thought-control today. Political correctness ("racial overtones" indeed!), with its selective agenda of bigotry to be condemned as against that to be tolerated or dismissed, with its power to explain away what elsewhere it finds intolerable—that political correctness is exposed in these pages.

Its affect upon the academy, its corruption of the very character of academic research in history and other humanities, as well as in the social sciences—none can now foresee the long-term effects of political correctness. But those of us who remember what 12 years of Nazism did to the German universities—the death of intellect, the end of integrity—cannot look with much confidence into the future of those many, formerly elite American universities that are complicit in the sad story told in these pages. Nazism left German universities empty of all intellectual vitality. With investigating committees proliferating and free speech now subject to violent challenge on our campuses, who can tell me how our universities differ from those of Nazi Germany, except in the detail that there the right defined the norm and here the left does? There the Jews were evicted, here those not among the scheduled castes—those not black, not female, not Latino, not homosexual, to name only the more prominent ones—are repressed. Objective accomplishment carries little weight, correct credentials prevail. How did Soviet and Nazi universities differ? And with the future of the humanities and most of the social sciences now in the hands of the ideologists of caprice and special pleading, who can expect a future worthy of the disciplinary task?

Our future is upon us. To defend King's plagiarism, plagiarism finds itself cleaned up and made a virtue of blacks, as exemplified by the theories of Keith Miller. As Pappas explains Miller's line of reasoning, "King's plagiarisms must have derived from his inability to separate himself from this [black] homiletic tradition [of plagia-rism] and to comprehend the standards of an alien 'white' culture." The academy, therefore, must now redefine plagiarism to accom-modate these "excluded" groups. So we have sunk to this! King does not deserve so shameful a defense. I believe Martin Luther King, Jr., was a man of conscience and character—but flesh and blood, like the rest of us. Those who thought to protect his name through deceit have traduced the man's own highest ideals, and did so, by excusing the inexcusable, in a way that ultimately diminished the stature and impoverished the heritage of a great man.

Nor can we readily distinguish between those who make excuses for plagiarists of a particular race or class and those who justify the ex-clusion of one race or class from the opportunities offered by an open society. Racism is racism, whether practiced by Nazis against Jews or by whites against blacks, and the stigmata of racism, de-fending in the other what one would not tolerate in oneself, finding reasons for the lapses of the lesser sorts—these evils abound in the controversy narrated in this book. King's condescending defenders, not his critics, are the racists.

The intellect always contains within itself the power of its own re-newal; reason does endure autonomous of the social order; persuasion compels, and argument changes minds. So the present corruption of intellect and its principal institutions cannot continue for very long. A hundred years from now, when issues other than race will per-force occupy this country of ours, what will people remember of the sorry record set forth here? I hope that someone will remember, in those days, that there was a man of sufficiently clear vision to see what counted: "It was Boston University's reputation, not Mr. King's, that was riding on the committee's handling of this controversy. We all know what King did; the only question was whether B.U. as an institution devoted to the pursuit of truth would have the honesty and integrity to admit its mistakes and acknowledge King's wrong-doings." In those few pure and simple phrases Pappas states all that the academy is supposed to represent. What a compliment he pays to us: "pursuit of truth . . . honesty and integrity . . . admit mistakes . . . acknowledge wrongdoings . . ."! Where else in our society do people address such expectations?

My own experience through a long academic career has taught this simple lesson: truth-telling is sometimes tough but always free of costs, but lying—though easy to accomplish—exacts an awful charge. I would not want it said, a century from now, that there was no one willing to stand by Theodore Pappas in his advocacy of the integrity of the academy and equal treatment of the races. That is why I am proud to invite readers to his book, and so to take my place beside the man possessed of the integrity to state, "In better days the follies of our heroes did not move us to subvert the moral underpinnings of our culture."

Those who share memories of an earlier age and understand the effect of the phrase "Senator, have you no shame?" will hear the echo today: "Professor, have you no shame?" And remembering the sounds of another day they will know what has changed—and what has stayed the same.

JACOB NEUSNER
Distinguished Research Professor of Religious Studies,
University of South Florida
Life Member of Clare Hall,
Cambridge University

INTRODUCTION

"Plagiarism, Culture, and the Future of the Academy" by Theodore Pappas

This essay first appeared in the December 1993 issue (Vol. 6, No. 2) of Humanitas, *a publication of the National Humanities Institute.*

In the 1980's it was still possible to defend proudly and with impunity the traditional definition of plagiarism and the commonsensical delineation of scholarly standards and responsibilities. Take, for example, Peter Shaw's 1982 essay on "Plagiary" in the *American Scholar.* His contention and conclusion were simple and straightforward, that a plagiarist remains as Lord Chesterfield described him, "a man that steals other people's thoughts and puts 'em off for his own"; that "literary critics and scholars must bear the responsibility to affirm that there is indeed such a thing as plagiarism and that they are capable of identifying it if necessary"; and that "the attempt to evade professional responsibility when a case of plagiarism arises only makes for further complications."[1] Thomas Mallon echoed these traditionalist views in *Stolen Words: Forays into the Origins and Ravages of Plagiarism* (1989).[2] But the cultural climate has changed, even since the 1980's, and defenders of literary standards and contemners of plagiarism now stand in stark contrast to the writers, scholars, editors, and publishers who have abandoned their responsibility as critics and watchdogs, forgone the unpleasantness of upholding propriety, and opted instead for a kinder and gentler conception of plagiarism that facilitates life for pilferer and critic alike. According to this "new thinking" about literary theft, plagiarism must go the way of other taboos that have been modified and redefined in deference to sensitivity and social progress.

To appreciate the gravity of this situation, it is important to understand, one, that plagiarism remains a serious social and cultural problem; two, that the current push to redefine plagiarism is directly tied to how famous cases of pilfering have been handled and mishandled throughout recent history; and, three, that at issue here is not just the definition of literary theft but the conceptions of authorship and originality on which scholarship and composition have been based for two centuries.

That plagiarism is relevant to our times can hardly be disputed. Senator Joseph Biden's bid for the presidency ended after he plagiarized a speech by British Labour Party leader Neil Kinnock in 1987. We now know that Martin Luther King, Jr., routinely plagiarized not only his college, seminary, and graduate school essays, including his doctoral dissertation, but many of his most famous speeches and published works as well, including the legendary "I Have a Dream" oration. "Plagiarism and Theft of Ideas" was the exclusive topic of the June 1993 conference of the American Association for the Advancement of Science. A 1990-1991 study by Donald McCabe of the Center for Academic Integrity indicates that over a third of undergraduates now admittedly plagiarize. Over the last decade or so plagiarism scandals and controversies have embroiled some of the most popular authors and their most popular works, including Alex Haley, for his Pulitzer Prize-winning *Roots*; Dee Brown, for *Bury My Heart at Wounded Knee*; Gail Sheehy, for *Passages*; Ken Follett, for *The Key to Rebecca*; Norman Mailer, for his biography of Marilyn Monroe; Jacob Epstein, for his novel *Wild Oats*; Joe McGinniss, for his recently released book on Teddy Kennedy, *The Last Brother*; David Leavitt, for his new novel *While England Sleeps*; and Maya Angelou, for her much-heralded "Inaugural Poem."[3]

Fraud and plagiarism in the literary, scientific, and scholarly worlds are more prominent and prolific than generally realized, and the way in which many cases of impropriety have been ignored, whitewashed, and covered up by the press, by editors, by publishers, and by universities has only aggravated the problem and encouraged such perfidy. Historian Stephen Nissenbaum spent years trying to convince both publishers and universities that his book *Sex, Diet, and Debility in Jacksonian America* had been brazenly plagiarized by a young historian at Texas Tech named Jayme Sokolow. As Nissenbaum wrote in the March 28, 1990, issue of the *Chronicle of Higher Education*, "though Mr. Sokolow's activities first came to light nine years ago . . . not one of the institutions that have learned of them has openly condemned what he did. That includes two universities, at least seven publishing houses, and three major national organizations."[4] Though Professor Nissenbaum finally succeeded in publicizing the theft, students can still find Sokolow's *Eros and Modernization* right alongside Nissenbaum's legitimately researched book in the library, the two works now shelved together because of the "similarity" of their topics.

A new controversy in the field of American history is brewing over the charges of Walter Stewart and Ned Feder of the National Institutes of Health. Stewart and Feder became famous (or notorious) in the mid-1980's, when their research uncovered serious fraud in the sciences, and since then they have devised a computerized method of detecting plagiarism. Last spring they filed with the American Historical Association a 1,400-page report on the alleged plagiarisms of historian and best-selling biographer Stephen Oates. According to the *Chicago Tribune* (May 10, 1993), the association has admitted to improper citations in Oates' biography of Abraham Lincoln but refused to call them plagiarism.[5] The new evidence reportedly demonstrates widespread plagiarisms throughout Oates' biographies of William Faulkner and Martin Luther King as well. The charge is serious and potentially damaging to the profession, as Oates' writings have long been staples of college courses in American history.

Nor have university administrators escaped such contretemps. In May 1991, the dean of Boston University's College of Communication, H. Joachim Maitre, delivered what many observers called a moving and powerful commencement address. It focused on how movies and television glorify both the ugly and the beautiful at the expense of religion and traditional values. There was only one problem: Dean Maitre had taken significant sections of the speech virtually verbatim from an article by film critic Michael Medved. Considering that Medved's article had already appeared in the *Wall Street Journal* and *Reader's Digest*—two more widely circulated publications could hardly be found—the dean's actions left commentators wondering whether plagiarism constituted the real offense. As Francis Getliffe suggests in C.P. Snow's novel *The Affair*, which deals with a case of scientific fraud, "there are times when stupidity seems to me the greater crime."[6]

In light of the Maitre incident and the controversy over the thesis that Martin Luther King plagiarized at Boston University in 1955, one might think that an encyclopedia's entry on "Plagiarism" would today end with the words "See also 'Boston University,'" but there is and has been plenty of chicanery on our campuses to go around. Regarding plagiarism in particular, the University of Oregon perhaps takes the gold. As the *New York Times* reported on June 6, 1980:

> Stanford University said today it had learned that its teaching assistant's handbook section on plagiarism had been plagiarized by the University of Oregon. Stanford issued a release saying Oregon officials conceded that the plagiarism section and other parts of its handbook were identical with the Stanford guidebook. Oregon officials apologized and said they would revise their guidebook.[7]

Of course, cribbing a faculty handbook is hardly an offense of staggering cultural consequence, but there are signs of more serious fraud, deception, and plagiarism among academics that seldom receive much press and scrutiny. This seems especially true with regard to the sciences, as a number of recent studies indicate. We have tended to view scientists since the Civil War and particularly in this century as paragons of objectivity and as champions of truth who are selfless in motivation, dispassionate in research, and immune to the lure of coin and convention. Just how often this image falls short of reality is now painfully clear. The investigations of Stewart and Feder, for example, were indispensable in uncovering the extent of the transgressions in the now-famous cases of John Darsee of the Harvard Medical School (the widely acclaimed rising star of biomedical research who, after publishing 122 journal articles in a little over two years, was found to have faked data in nearly every paper) and of Dr. David Baltimore (the Nobel Prize-winning scientist who signed on to and then embarrassingly defended to the eleventh hour an article based on faked data).

The potential danger of such fraud cannot be overstated. Robert Bell, in *Impure Science: Fraud, Compromise, and Political Influence in Scientific Research* (1992), cites the example of Dr. Stephen Breuning of the University of Pittsburgh Medical School, who pleaded guilty in September 1988 to two charges of filing fake reports on projects funded with federal money.[8] The bogus reports had not only been relied on nationwide for determining drug therapy for severely retarded and institutionalized children, but they had even endorsed and recommended the exact opposite treatment from that proven sound and safe by legitimate studies. Marcel C. LaFollette, in *Stealing into Print: Fraud, Plagiarism, and Misconduct in Scientific Publishing* (1992), echoes Bell's concern and shows how the peer-review process and political grandstanding have greatly hindered attempts to crack down on fraud and plagiarism. The latter now appears to be the more prevalent form of malfeasance. "Both the NSF [the National Science Foundation] and NIH [National Institutes of Health] now report that they investigate substantially more allegations involving plagiarism and stolen ideas than allegations involving falsified or altered data," she notes.[9]

Even the grand old man of the sea—Jacques Cousteau—appears to fall short of our vision of the sainted scientist. French journalist Bernard Violet, in *Cousteau: A Biography* (1992), has touched off a fierce controversy in his country with his contention that numerous sea scenes in Cousteau's movies were secretly staged in a Marseilles studio, that divers faked illnesses and equipment failure for dramatic effect, and that animals were purposely harmed to induce a desired response for the camera. Now, the possible torture of sea animals is hardly germane to a discussion of plagiarism, but what is certainly relevant is how Violet felt upon uncovering such inglorious information about a man whom he and his countrymen have long revered as a national icon. The shock and disappointment he experienced are, in fact, similar to that which Clayborne Carson, the editor of the King Papers Project at Stanford University, reportedly felt upon learning of the evidence of Martin Luther King's plagiarisms. "I had admired Cousteau since the age of seven," says Violet, "when my father took me to see *Le monde du silence*, Cousteau's first film and winner of the Cannes Film Festival in 1956. Now I feel like an orphan."[10]

Orphans are often found in the wake of famous plagiarism scandals, and the disillusionment they experience is nothing to take lightly, as I learned firsthand. The occasion was a Chicago talk-radio show in the fall of 1990. I was being interviewed about an article of mine on King's plagiarized dissertation, which at the time was the only article to describe in detail how and what King had pilfered. My argument was twofold: that, regardless of how one felt about King's historic role as leader of a social movement, his blatant plagiarizing in pursuit of America's highest academic degree—specifically, his stealing of large sections of a dissertation by Jack Boozer—was an indefensible act that should warrant the revocation of his Ph.D.; and that Boston University could posthumously award King an honorary doctorate for his contribution to civil rights but that it had an obligation as an institution devoted to the pursuit of truth to revile and revoke what was fraudulently earned. One female caller's response: "People like you should be 'taken out'!" And she did not mean to dinner and a movie.

This woman's impulse to behead (in my case, perhaps literally) the bearer of the bad news instead of dealing with the bad news itself is a feature common to famous plagiarism cases since the time of Coleridge. Why the age of Coleridge, the late 18th and early 19th centuries, is relevant to this discussion may not be obvious without remembering when the idea of plagiarism first began to challenge the classical notion of imitation that had long reigned in the West as the preferred method of composition. As George Kennedy explains in *Classical Rhetoric and Its Christian and Secular Tradition from Ancient to Modern Times* (1980), classical writing and oratory were

> to a considerable extent a pastiche, or piecing together of commonplaces, long or short. . . . The student memorized passages as he would letters and made up a speech out of these elements as he would words out of letters. . . . In the Middle Ages handbooks of letter-writing often contained formulae, such as openings and closes, which the student could insert into a letter, and a whole series of formulary

rhetorics existed in the Renaissance.[11]

Rhetoricians, however, expected these models, formulae, pastiches, and commonplaces to be recognized by their auditors and accepted for what they were—either clichés of basic oratory or time-honored excerpts of the masters. There was no attempt to deceive or to pass off the genius of others as one's own, which, of course, a plagiarist aims to do. As Seneca the Elder said of Ovid, "as he had done with many other lines of Virgil [he] borrowed the idea, not desiring to deceive people, but to have it openly recognized as borrowed."[12]

This classical tradition of imitation was not significantly challenged until the 18th century. It was then that authorship, originality, and plagiarism became for the first time prime issues of debate, and by the age of Coleridge and Romanticism, an obsession with originality and a fanatical crediting of literary property had become defining features of Western culture. This development was not to everyone's liking. Tennyson was appalled by the "prosaic set growing up among us—editors of booklets, bookworms, index-hunters, or men of great memories . . . [that] will not allow one to say, 'Ring the bell' without finding that we have taken it from Sir P. Sidney, or even to use such a simple expression as the ocean 'roars' without finding out the precise verse in Homer or Horace from which we have plagiarized it."[13] This "prosaic set" that Tennyson, Pope, and others railed against was the new breed of scholar—the "pedants without insight, intellectuals without love"—who trivialized literature, distorted aesthetics, and sought prestige and honor not through originality but by impugning the originality of men of proven talent.

The other factor contributing to this heightened concern for authorship stemmed from a socioeconomic, not aesthetic, change: the profitability of putting pen to pad had given rise to that dubious lot of "Grub Street" scribblers known as professional writers. It is not surprising, then, that the first detailed discussions and definitions of plagiarism issue from this period and from the likes of Johnson, Pope, Goldsmith, and De Quincey. Thomas Mallon, in *Stolen Words*, describes the transition this way:

A modern world was printing and distributing itself into

existence. Literary "careers" would be "made," and writerly goods would get sold, not because they were skillful variants of earlier ones but because they were *original*. . . . Eventually a bourgeois world would create its own new genre, the novel, and authors would be brand names, the "new Scott" asked for like this year's carriage model.[14]

It is also at this time that we find an increased interest in the detection of forged documents and the first serious calls for copyright statutes.

The continuity between this period and our own in the handling of famous cases of plagiarism can most readily be seen by juxtaposing two of the most prominent filchers of the last two centuries: Samuel Taylor Coleridge and Martin Luther King, Jr. That Coleridge boldly plagiarized—not in his famous poems but most blatantly in his *Biographia Literaria* and in his lectures on Shakespeare—is still not widely known among the general public. What Peter Shaw wrote 12 years ago in the *American Scholar* remains largely true:

> Today the general reading public remains for the most part unaware that Coleridge was a plagiarist, while literary critics and professors of English—outside of those who specialize in the study of Romantic poetry—are largely unaware of the extent and significance of his plagiarism. The manner in which the present state of ignorance came about bears directly on the literary world's current unwillingness to deal with contemporary cases of plagiarism.[15]

Though these two men differ in ways that are as numerous as they are obvious, their similarities as plagiarists are nevertheless striking and useful for highlighting how famous cases of pilfering typically play out. Both men plagiarized some of their most influential prose and were publicly exposed as pilferers only after death. The plagiarisms of both men were widely rumored and whispered about prior to their exposure and were secretly known by numerous individuals who suppressed the story. Both men had spirited celebrants for whom no excuse, justification, or rationalization was too fantastic to enlist in the defense of their hero's work and reputation. And both men publicly defended their purloined property as their own.

The apologists' ingenious attempts to palliate the plagiarisms can be entertaining. Both Thomas Mallon and Peter Shaw summarize the arguments of Coleridge's principal defenders. In rebutting J.C. Ferrier's relentless documentation of Coleridge's thefts, for example, Thomas McFarland contends that "it is surprising and rather anti-climactic to find that when the firing is over Ferrier has discovered no more than nineteen pages of plagiarism in the hundreds that make up the *Biographia Literaria*."[16] The committee that Boston University convened to investigate King's plagiarisms adopts a similar argu-ment in its September 1991 report. Because King stole only 45 per-cent of his thesis's first half, and only 21 percent of the second, the dissertation remains an "intelligent contribution to scholarship," and "no thought should be given to the revocation of Dr. King's doc-toral degree."[17] As Peter Shaw wondered in regard to McFarland's de-fense, "If nineteen pages are anticlimactic, it is not clear what would have impressed McFarland in the circumstances—twenty-one pages copied? Twenty-five? Fifty?"[18] Similarly with Boston University's handling of King's plagiarisms. What kind of numbers would have to be posted to impress that university? Say, plagiarism covering 65 percent of the first half and 45 percent of the second?

McFarland refers to Coleridge's "mode of composition—compo-sition by mosaic organization." This language is similar to Walter Jackson Bate's and James Engell's comparison of Coleridge's plagia-risms to "a chemical compound." But such phrases are merely eu-phemisms for plagiarism. They are typical of the rhetorical muf-flers with which apologists for plagiarists swathe and bedizen themselves in an effort to suppress the cold reality of theft. At one point Clayborne Carson even forbad everyone at the King Papers Project at Stanford to utter the dreaded "p-word." He spoke instead of "similarities," "paraphrasing," and "textual appropriations" as part of King's "successful composition method." To the credit of the *Journal of American History*, when Carson submitted an article about King's plagiarisms that was replete with duplicity of this kind, the journal rejected it for disingenuousness, for a lack of forthrightness with the truth. But Carson, Bate, Engell, and McFarland are neophytes in comparison with the versatile Keith Miller of Arizona State University, a professor of English and the author of *Voice of Deliverance: The Language of Martin Luther King, Jr., and Its Sources* (1992).[19] Though Miller's research is indispensable for ascertaining the sources of stolen material in King's most famous speeches and published works, it employs rhetorical tricks and semantical sophistry to an extraordinary extent. King's pirating was not "plagiarism," but rather "voice merging," "intertextualizations," "incorporations," "borrowings," "consulting," "absorbing," "alchemizing," "overlapping," "quarrying," "yoking," "adopting," "synthesizing," "replaying," "echoing," "resonances," and "reverberations."

Bate and Engell eventually rely on the most time-honored excuse for plagiarism, that the improprieties were unintentional and merely stemmed from careless notetaking and hasty writing. Surprisingly, historian Eugene Genovese adopts this very line in his exculpation of King. While acknowledging the thefts—often verbatim thefts of entire paragraphs—that King committed throughout college and graduate school, Professor Genovese (in the May 11, 1992, issue of the *New Republic*) discounts their significance and argues that King simply "misquoted in a manner that suggests impatience with scholarly procedures," a "sloppiness" that was "not an expression of laziness or an unwillingness to do the required work."[20] When verbatim plagiarism became a legitimate way of doing "the required work" at our universities—let alone a method of completing a doctoral dissertation, which by definition means an original work of scholarship—and how an "impatience with scholarly standards" accounts for the plagiarisms King committed throughout the decade and a half after he left academia, Professor Genovese does not say. What could have affected the judgment of so fine a scholar?

S. Paul Schilling, who was the second reader of King's dissertation at Boston University, follows a similar path of palliation. As he states in a letter that the university reproduces in its September 1991 report, "it should be recognized [that King] was operating on a very crowded schedule during most of the work on his dissertation," as if plagiarism is acceptable or at least excusable if one is busy and in a hurry. Schilling adds, "it should be recognized that [King's] appropriation of the language of others does not entail inaccurate interpretation of the thought of writers cited."[21] Apparently a plagiarist deserves praise for stealing accurately.

Another characteristic common to plagiarism cases is the role and fate of the exposer of the misdeeds. When in Rex Stout's *Plot It Yourself* Nero Wolfe's assistant interrogates a literary agent about a case of "plagiarism upside down"—the planting of a back-dated manuscript of a published work for purposes of blackmailing the legitimate author as a plagiarist—he senses "from [the agent's] tone that anyone who made a plagiarism claim was a louse."[22] Here, in a nutshell, is the typical fate of the whistleblower. No one suffers the pangs and arrows of outrageous fortune like the exposer of a famous plagiarist, for it is he, not the sinner and certainly not the sin, who becomes the center of debate, the target of abuse, and the victim of the hot and harsh lights of public scrutiny. Walter Stewart and Ned Feder know this all too well. On May 10, 1993, the National Institutes of Health confiscated their files and computer terminals and discs, forbad them to address the issue of plagiarism for the foreseeable future, and reassigned them to such tasks as folding protein before placing them on leave. "My partner was told," Stewart told the *Chicago Tribune* (May 10, 1993), "that it would be inappropriate for him to comment on any errors or problems he might see in published scientific literature. We think that's just what someone who monitors research projects funded with the government's money ought to be doing."[23] And what precipitated this clampdown? It seems pressure was exerted on NIH via a tie to the Clinton administration, a person close to one of the scholars Stewart and Feder recently investigated. A better example of political intrigue could hardly be found, and yet the story remains buried.

Of course, the "burying" of the unpalatable and politically sensitive is hardly an anomaly in American journalism. Thanks to Charles Babington's article "Embargoed" in the January 28, 1991, issue of the *New Republic*, we now know that numerous publications—including the *New York Times*, the *Washington Post*, the *Atlanta Journal/Constitution*, as well as the *New Republic*—had long known about King's thefts but deliberately suppressed the story.[24] *Chronicles: A Magazine of American Culture* first became interested in the story in mid-1990, when it received, accepted, and set for publication a short article from a scholar praising King and the civil rights movement but mild-ly rebuking him for plagiarizing his dissertation. The author, how-ever, pulled the piece at the last moment. It was then—when faced with the clear sign that this story and its serious ramifications were not going to be tackled by the academic community—that I or-dered the two dissertations and went public with detailed evidence of King's plagiarisms.

The reader might think that, after two centuries, the conven-tional conceptions of literary property and literary theft would be safely and securely embedded in our culture and beyond reproach, di-lution, or subversion. As Thomas Mallon wrote in 1989, "Original-ity—not just innocence of plagiarism but the making of something really and truly new—set itself down as a cardinal literary virtue sometime in the middle of the eighteenth century and has never since gotten up."[25] Unfortunately, we now encounter challenges from within the academy itself to subvert the traditional concep-tions of authorship and originality that have persevered for two cen-turies as the standards for scholarship and composition. Most dis-turbing, this potential paradigm shift of serious consequence is occurring amid the silence of the scholarly community.

What Professor Mallon could not have foreseen is the rise of Keith Miller and his application of the new "voice merging" theory. Miller contends that plagiarism by certain minorities should not be condemned but rather "understood" in the context of their cultural experience. For example, because King was black as well as a preach-er, and because black preachers have traditionally "voice merged" with one another by freely swapping sermons without attribution, Miller concludes that King's plagiarisms must have derived from an inability to distinguish the classroom from the pulpit, to separate himself from this homiletic tradition, and to comprehend the stan-dards of an alien white culture—still apparently alien to King after 11 years of higher education (often at predominantly white institu-tions), three academic degrees, and a graduate school seminar on plagiarism and scholarly standards. Miller extrapolates from this reasoning that, since many minorities come from cultures rich in oral traditions, we must redefine plagiarism to accommodate these "excluded" groups. Put more bluntly, all legal claims to original thought and the interpretation of ideas must now yield in deference to multiculturalism, diversity, cultural relativism, and human rights. As Miller argues in "Redefining Plagiarism" in the January 20, 1993, issue of the *Chronicle of Higher Education*, "the process of securing fundamental human rights such as those King championed— outweighs the right to the exclusive use of intellectual and literary property."[26]

Miller's second reason for wanting to redefine plagiarism stems specifically from King's pilfering. "We face a contradiction," he suggests in his essay. "We wish to lionize a man for his powerful language while decrying a major strategy that made his words resonate and persuade." Miller then issues a startling non sequitur: "How could such a compelling leader commit what most people define as a writer's worst sin? The contradiction should prompt us to rethink our definition of plagiarism."[27] Should we also rethink drunk driving in light of Chappaquiddick and redefine adultery to account for King's philandering?

Apparently Miller is not alone in holding such views. In fact, one professor in the February 24, 1993, issue of the *Chronicle of Higher Education* not only praised Miller's essay but regretted that he "did not go far enough." For "when the purpose is to use ideas—for inspiration, practical value, clarity of purpose, good fellowship, or whatever—it can only hinder us to wonder who deserves credit for them."[28] Clayborne Carson wrote in a similar vein in the January 16, 1991, issue of the *Chronicle of Higher Education*. While "recognizing that textual appropriation was one aspect of [King's] successful composition method," King's "legitimate utilization of political, philosophical, and literary texts—particularly those expressing the nation's democratic ideals—inspired and mobilized many Americans, thereby advancing the cause of social justice."[29] Such statements, in essence, say the end justifies the means, that if one steals for the right reason—whatever "right" may be, as defined by whomever—then the vice is excusable if not sanctionable and commendable. Note the publication in which these arguments have appeared. Sinons with Trojan horses have clearly passed through the gates of academe.

Transforming plagiarism into a virtue in light of King's pilfering is

Miller's aim. He accomplishes this goal through three stages in his book. He first sets the "proper" tone by opening with an epigraph from Quintilian—the first-century rhetorician whose *Institutio Oratoria* is the masterwork on the subject of classical imitation.[30] The implication is clear, that both his arguments and King's plagiarisms are nothing more than a continuation of a hallowed Western tradition. His "voice merging" theory follows and prepares the reader for his bold conclusion: that King's plagiarisms were perhaps his greatest gift to the country. For by "intertextualizing" stolen works into his popular speeches and essays, and by stealing in particular the words and writings of liberal white preachers, King "foolproofed his discourse" and was able to "change the minds of moderate and uncommitted whites" toward solving "the nation's most horrific problem—racial injustice." In fact, "Not only did voice merging keep Jefferson's dream alive, it also helped compel the White House to withdraw from the nightmare of Vietnam. Then in the wake of his movement came the second wave of American feminism, the campaign for gay rights, and the crusade to save the environment."[31] All this owed to plagiarism! Miller offers, however, no proof whatsoever that King intentionally plagiarized white sources or that he did so specifically to further the aims and popularity of the civil rights movement.

Miller's ideas are spreading among minority groups and are now even vying for legal sanction. "A lawyer asked me for advice in defending a Native American student charged with plagiarizing papers in law school," he writes in the *Chronicle of Higher Education*. "The student came from an oral culture, and could not immediately understand or obey the rules of written English. . . . King's example thus is not an isolated case."[32] Indeed, the number of such cases will doubtless multiply: "voice merging" is a godsend to plagiarist and lawyer alike.

To the hundreds of individuals who have asked me in recent years, in prosecutorial tone, why I or anyone should be interested in plagiarism and in the Martin Luther King, Jr., plagiarism story in particular, I point out that, in the country with ostensibly the freest and most adversarial press in the world, many of our leading journals and newspapers knew about King's plagiarisms and the extent of the transgressions but deliberately spiked and suppressed the story; that Keith Miller and his followers and their propositions, if left unchallenged and allowed to root, will undermine scholarship and composition as traditionally conceived; and that Clayborne Carson and the King Papers staff uncovered evidence of King's plagiarisms in 1987, misrepresented the evidence to the public for three years thereafter, and—after eight years on the public payroll as editors and scholars with nearly a million dollars of the taxpayers' money via the National Endowment for the Humanities—have still published only one volume of an expected 14-volume set.

But there is a deeper, more significant reason to be interested in this story. As Anthony Grafton of Princeton University eloquently concludes in *Forgers and Critics: Creativity and Duplicity in Western Scholarship* (1990), "The exercise of criticism is a sign of health and virtue in a civilization; the prevalence of forgery is a sign of illness and vice."[33] What Professor Grafton states about forgery holds equally true for plagiarism, and considering the duplicity, disingenuousness, and disrespect for free debate that now are overwhelming our approach to criticism and higher learning, it would be wise to heed Professor Grafton's remarks. Harboring fraud and deception is bad enough. Calling them scholarship and truth signals the end of the academy and intellectual discourse as we know them.

NOTES

1. Peter Shaw, "Plagiary," *American Scholar* (Summer 1982), 325-337.
2. Thomas Mallon, *Stolen Words: Forays into the Origins and Ravages of Plagiarism* (New York: Ticknor and Fields, 1989).
3. The last three examples—those of Joe McGinniss, David Leavitt, and Maya Angelou—are breaking stories that developed as we went to press. For discussions of these controversies, see, respectively, Tom Fitzpatrick's "That's Spelled P-L-A-G-I-A-R-I-S-M" in the Phoenix *New Times*, September 1-7, 1993; Andrei Navrozov's "The Age of Plagiarism" in *The Times Magazine* of London, October 2, 1993; and John Meroney's "Maya Angelou's Inaugural

Poem: Plagiarized or Inspired?" in *Chronicles*, December 1993.

4. Stephen Nissenbaum, "The Plagiarists in Academe Must Face Formal Sanctions," *Chronicle of Higher Education* (28 March 1990), A52.

5. Ron Grossman, "Silencing the Whistle: Plagiarism Cops Lose Their License to Embarrass," *Chicago Tribune* (10 May 1993), Tempo Section, 1. For a more detailed discussion of the Oates controversy, see Peter Shaw's "The Fatal Pattern of Plagiary" in the August & September 1991 edition of *Illinois Issues*.

6. C.P. Snow, *The Affair* (New York: Charles Scribner's Sons, 1960), 123.

7. "Plagiarism Book is Plagiarized," *New York Times* (6 June 1980), A28.

8. Robert Bell, *Impure Science: Fraud, Compromise, and Political Influence in Scientific Research* (New York: John Wiley & Sons, Inc., 1992), 105-110.

9. Marcel C. LaFollette, *Stealing into Print: Fraud, Plagiarism, and Misconduct in Scientific Publishing* (Berkeley: University of California Press, 1992), 48-49.

10. From a 1993 interview of Bernard Violet by Pierre Prier of *The European*.

11. George A. Kennedy, *Classical Rhetoric and Its Christian and Secular Tradition from Ancient to Modern Times* (Chapel Hill: University of North Carolina, 1980), 28-29.

12. *The Suasoriae of Seneca the Elder*, iii, 7. Quoted in Harold Ogden White, *Plagiarism and Imitation During the English Renaissance: A Study in Critical Distinctions* (Cambridge: Harvard University Press, 1935), 5-6.

13. From a 24 November 1882 letter to Mrs. S.E. Dawson. See Sir Edward Cook, *More Literary Recreations* (London: The Macmillan Company, 1919), 177-184 and Alexander Lindey, *Plagiarism and Originality* (New York: Harper & Brothers Publishers, 1952), 52-53.

14. Mallon, *Stolen Words*, 5.

15. Shaw, "Plagiary," 334.

16. *Ibid.*, 335.

17. "Report of the Boston University Committee to Investigate

Charges of Plagiarism in the Ph.D. Dissertation of Martin Luther King, Jr." (September 1991), 2-4.

18. Shaw, "Plagiary," 335.
19. Keith D. Miller, *Voice of Deliverance: The Language of Martin Luther King, Jr. and Its Sources* (New York: The Free Press, 1992).
20. Eugene D. Genovese, "Pilgrim's Progress," *New Republic* (11 May 1992), 35.
21. "Report of the Boston University Committee," Appendix D.
22. Rex Stout, *Plot It Yourself* (New York: The Viking Press, 1959), 164.
23. Grossman, *Chicago Tribune*, Tempo Section, 3.
24. Charles Babington, "Embargoed," *New Republic* (28 January 1991), 9-11.
25. Mallon, *Stolen Words*, 24.
26. Miller, "Redefining Plagiarism: Martin Luther King's Use of an Oral Tradition," *Chronicle of Higher Education* (20 January 1993), A60.
27. *Ibid.*
28. Ken Lebensold, "Plagiarism, Copyright, and Ownership of Ideas," *Chronicle of Higher Education* (24 February 1993), B4.
29. Clayborne Carson, "Documenting Martin Luther King's Importance—and His Flaws," *Chronicle of Higher Education* (16 January 1991), A52.
30. See in particular Book X of Quintilian's *Institutio Oratoria*.
31. Miller, *Voice of Deliverance*, 195.
32. Miller, "Redefining Plagiarism," A60.
33. Anthony Grafton, *Forgers and Critics: Creativity and Duplicity in Western Scholarship* (Princeton: Princeton University Press, 1990), 127.

ONE

"Martin Luther King—Was He a Plagiarist?" by Frank Johnson

Frank Johnson's article in the London Sunday Telegraph *on December 3, 1989, was the first discussion in a major newspaper of the then "rumor" of King's plagiarisms. It appeared in Mr. Johnson's regular diary column called "Mandrake" and is reprinted here with permission.*

Researchers in his native Georgia must soon decide whether to reveal that the late Dr. Martin Luther King, murdered in 1968, was—in addition to his other human failings—a plagiarist. There is now much doubt as to whether his Ph.D. thesis was really his own work.

In my view this does not detract from his greatness, no more than did the revelations about his extramarital sex life. But it is causing anguish among scholars working on his collected papers and it is bound to be said either that the accusation is false or—if true—that it should not have been made known to the world.

The story has not yet been published in the United States. I heard about it from an American friend who learned it from one of the scholars now preparing the collection of speeches, sermons, academic papers and correspondence to be published in 12 volumes over the next 15 years. Volume one is to be published next autumn.

According to my informant, the associate editor of the project, Dr. Ralph Luker, of Emory University, has discovered that Dr. King's thesis at Boston University in the early 1950's—on the theological concept known as "personalism"—lent heavily on the work, a few years before, of a white student, Jack Boozer, who went on to become a professor at Emory. Professor Boozer died not long ago.

Apparently, King mentioned Boozer's work in a footnote, but did not indicate the extent to which the thesis came from him. When I telephoned Dr. Luker at Emory and asked whether it was true that Dr. King's thesis was plagiarized, he chose his words slowly and carefully. "I have no way of responding to that," he said. "We're in the process of conducting our research, and will be able to report on that research within the next nine months."

Did Dr. King acknowledge his indebtedness to another theologian? I asked. "There is a full bibliography in the dissertation," Dr. Luker replied.

Is the research team even considering the possibility of plagiarism? "It would be very foolish for us to attempt any kind of statement at this point," he replied, "because our research is not complete. When we think we know what the situation is, then we will be prepared to report it."

If plagiarism is discovered, would researchers have a duty to reveal it? "Our reputations as historians are on the line," said Dr. Luker. "I think you can draw the conclusion from that. If we thought we had a clear picture of the overall situation, and were certain of our grounds."

Dr. Clayborne Carson, of Stanford University, California, who is in overall charge of the project, said: "It's really not true" (that the thesis was plagiarized). But other remarks by him suggest that there is a problem. Asked whether the charge was completely without substance, he said: "It's hard to give a categorical answer. The answer to that question is 'no.' But it's still in the process. There is no fraud [in the dissertation]. What we're talking about is the question of whether there was adequate citation of all sources. . . . Right now, it's like calling an author before the manuscript is finished."

TWO

Excerpt from "Revolution and Tradition in the Humanities Curriculum" by Thomas Fleming

This paragraph from Thomas Fleming's essay in the September 1990 Chronicles *was the first mention of King's plagiarisms in the American press to garner national attention.*

Who has not heard story after story about conservative leaders who bought or "arranged" their doctorates, who were found guilty of plagiarism, perjury, or fraud? Perhaps this explains the new popularity that Dr. Martin Luther King enjoys among Big Government conservatives. The "Doctor" should now be understood as strictly a courtesy title, since King, it has been recently revealed, apparently plagiarized his Boston University doctoral dissertation. King's phoney Ph.D. is enough to make him a hero to at least one self-described "progressive" conservative foundation executive who bought his degree from a storefront diploma mill in Florida and now passes on academic grants that add up to millions every year. It is people like this who today control the conservative movement. If conservatives are serious about upholding the permanent things, then they should see to it that those who are holding this banner do not, by their character, incompetence, and behavior, disgrace it.

THREE

Letter from Jon Westling of Boston University to *Chronicles*

In response to Thomas Fleming's mention of King's plagiarisms, Boston University's acting president, Jon Westling, sent Chronicles *the following letter for publication. It is dated October 5, 1990, and appeared in the January 1991 issue of* Chronicles.

In "Revolution and Tradition in the Humanities Curriculum" (September 1990), Thomas Fleming repeats the false story that Dr. Martin Luther King, Jr., plagiarized his Boston University doctoral dissertation. The charge has been made several times in the last year and appears to be spreading like whooping cough among the unvaccinated. Allow me to introduce some penicillin.

Dr. King's dissertation has, in fact, been scrupulously examined and reexamined by scholars, including scholars who are thoroughly familiar with the "personalist" theological tradition to which Dr. King's dissertation was a contribution and who would stand the best chance of catching any nonattributed quotations. Not a single instance of plagiarism of any sort has been identified.

The apparent source of this defamatory rumor was an article that appeared last December in a London newspaper—an article that was refuted by its supposed primary source in a subsequent issue. To my knowledge, the reappearance of this rumor in a recent issue of *Chronicles* is the first time that any reputable journal has stumbled into this pseudo-controversy.

To set the record straight, since 1955, when Dr. King submitted his dissertation, "A Comparison of the Conceptions of God in the Thinking of Paul Tillich and Henry Nelson Wieman," not a single reader has ever found any nonattributed or misattributed quotations, misleading paraphrases, or thoughts borrowed without due scholarly reference in any of its 343 pages. If you or anyone else have evidence to the contrary, it should be presented.

FOUR

"A Doctor in Spite of Himself: The Strange Career of Martin Luther King, Jr.'s Dissertation"
by Theodore Pappas

The following article was Chronicles' *response to Mr. Westling. It ran in the same issue in which Mr. Westling's letter appeared, the January 1991 number. The issue was sent to press on October 25, 1990, two weeks before the* Wall Street Journal's *front-page story about King's plagiarisms. When the* Journal's *story appeared on November 9,* Chronicles *hurriedly added an "update" to the article and circulated advanced copies. The article was widely quoted and discussed in such publications as the* Washington Post *and* Chicago Tribune, *the* Chronicle of Higher Education *and the* Journal of American History. *It was the first article to present detailed evidence of King's plagiarisms.*

On December 3, 1989, the *Sunday Telegraph* in London included a piece of academic news from the United States: "Researchers in his native Georgia must soon decide whether to reveal that the late Dr. Martin Luther King, murdered in 1968, was—in addition to his other human failings—a plagiarist. There is now much doubt as to whether his Ph.D. thesis was really his own work." This story had been making the rounds in academic circles for quite some time, but, as the *Telegraph* correctly added, "The story has not yet been published in the United States."

King received a Boston University Ph.D. in theology for a 1955 dissertation entitled "A Comparison of the Conceptions of God in the Thinking of Paul Tillich and Henry Nelson Wieman." According to the rumor, King's discussion of Tillich was based on a dissertation by one Jack Stewart Boozer entitled "The Place of Reason in Paul Tillich's Concept of God," for which Boozer was awarded a Ph.D. in theology from Boston University in 1952. Boozer, who later became a professor of theology at Emory University, died in 1989. Dr. Clayborne Carson of Stanford University, chief editor of the King Papers Project, quickly denied that there was any validity to the rumor, telling the *Telegraph*, "It's really not true [that the dissertation was plagiarized]." When pressed whether the charge against King was entirely without substance, he reportedly replied: "It's hard to give a categorical answer. . . .What we're talking about is the question of whether there was adequate citation of all sources."

Dr. Ralph Luker of Emory University, the associate editor of the King papers, told the *Telegraph* that a research team was considering the possibility of plagiarism. "We're in the process of conducting our research, and will be able to report on that research within the next nine months." "It would be very foolish for us to attempt any kind of statement at this point," he added, "because our research is not complete. When we think we know what the situation is, then we will be prepared to report it. . . . Our reputations as historians are on the line."

Despite the serious nature of the charge, more than nine months have passed and no scholarly article has appeared and no discussion of the charges has occurred in our nation's press. The question is, are we dealing with a substantial case of plagiarism or merely an instance of careless documentation? To begin with, it is worth noting that King's dissertation deals with many of the same topics found in Boozer's dissertation, and that King reaches virtually every conclusion that Boozer does concerning Tillich's conception of God—that Tillich's thought is often paradoxical if not contradictory, that Tillich sees God as "being-itself," that Tillich in the end affirms a monistic system of theology not entirely unlike Plotinus's and Hegel's, etc. Even so, it is possible to borrow a man's ideas, arguments, and evidence but paraphrase his actual language in a way that manages to stop short of plagiarism.

But, as Samuel Johnson made clear, when "there is a concurrence of more resemblances than can be imagined to have happened by chance; as where the same ideas are conjoined without any natural series or necessary coherence, or where not only the thought but the words are copied," plagiarism is surely present. This remains to date the best definition of plagiarism, and if we apply it to this case we must reach the inescapable conclusion that Mr. King committed plagiarism repeatedly in the course of his dissertation.

It is not merely that King's argument, language, and choice of words run parallel with Boozer's, but that whole phrases, sentences, and even paragraphs are lifted verbatim from Boozer's text. Dr. Luker of Emory is correct in pointing out that King acknowledges, on page five, that a "fine" dissertation was done on Tillich in 1952. And King does say on page seven that "the present inquiry will utilize from these valuable secondary sources any results which bear directly on the problem, and will indicate such use by appropriate footnotes." King, however, does not do this. In fact, among the dozens of sections he lifts from Boozer, he footnotes Boozer only twice, on pages 123 and 161—and then he gets both footnotes wrong (the first quote is found on page 193 of Boozer's text, not page 209; and the second on page 63, not page 62).

A wrong footnote here or an incorrect page number there would not warrant a discussion of plagiarism. But such slips are symptoms and signs of a much more serious offense. There is virtually no section of King's discussion of Tillich that cannot be found in Boozer's text, and often the parallels are not simply similarities but downright duplications. In other words, contrary to Dr. Carson's claim, what is involved here is by no means a mere matter of inadequate citation, as the following examples will make clear. The cumbersome footnotes King and Boozer make to Tillich's original texts have been excluded. In none of the following passages does King footnote Boozer. On the subject of the Trinity:

King:	Boozer:
For Tillich the trinity is not the illogical and irrational assertion that three are one and one is	The doctrine of the trinity is not the illogical assertion that three are one.

three. It is a qualitative rather than a quantitative characterization of God. It is an attempt to express the richness and complexity of the divine life. . . . It is the abysmal character of God, the element of power which is the basis of the Godhead, "which makes God God." (pp. 152-153)

Rather it is a qualitative characterization of God. It is an effort to express the richness of the divine life. . . . It is the abysmal character of God, the element of power, which is the basis of the Godhead, "which makes God God." (p. 214)

On dualism:

King:
[Dualism] is aware of the two poles of reality, but dualism conceives these in a static complementary relationship. Tillich maintains that these poles are related in dynamic interaction, that one pole never exists out of relation to the other pole. Herein is one of Tillich's basic criticisms of Hegel. Hegel, according to Tillich, transcends the tension of existential involvement in the concept of a synthesis. (p. 25)

Boozer:
Dualism is aware of the two poles of reality, but dualism conceives these in a static complementary relationship. Tillich maintains that they are related in a dynamic interaction, that one pole never exists out of relation to the other pole. One feels here again that . . . Tillich criticizes Hegel. For, according to Tillich, Hegel transcends the tension of existential involvement in the concept of a synthesis. (p. 268)

On God's manifestation in history:

King:
In a real sense, then,
God manifests himself
in history. This
manifestation is never
complete because God as
abyss is inexhaustible. But
God as *logos* is manifest
in history and is in real
interdependence with
man.
(p. 27)

Boozer:
In a real sense, then . . .
God manifests himself
in history. This
manifestation is never
complete because God as
abyss is inexhaustible. But
God as *logos* is manifest
in history and is in real
interdependence with
man and man's *logos*.
(p. 270)

On correlation:

King:
Correlation means
correspondence of data
in the sense of a
correspondence between
religious symbols and that
which is symbolized by
them. It is upon the
assumption of this
correspondence that all
utterances about God's
nature are made. This
correspondence is actual
in the logos nature of
God and the *logos* nature
of man. (p. 21)

Boozer:
Correlation means
correspondence of data
in the sense of a
correspondence between
religious symbols and that
which is symbolized by
them. It is upon the
assumption of this
correspondence that all
utterances about God's
nature are made. This
correspondence is actual
in the logos-nature of
God and the *logos*-nature
of man. (p. 265)

On another meaning of correlation:

King:
A second meaning of correlation is the logical interdependence of concepts. It is polar relationships that fall chiefly under this meaning of cor-relation. . . . The world does not stand by itself. Particular being is in correlation with being-itself. In this second meaning of correlation, then, Tillich moves beyond epistemological considerations to ontological considerations. (p. 24)

Boozer:
A second meaning of correlation is the logical interdependence of concepts. Tillich regards polar relationships as falling under this meaning of cor-relation. . . . The world does not stand by itself. Particular being is in correlation with being-itself. In the second meaning of correlation, then, Tillich moves beyond an epistemological consideration to a ontological consideration. (pp. 267-268)

On symbol and sign:

King:
A symbol possesses a necessary character. It cannot be exchanged. A sign, on the contrary, is impotent and can be exchanged at will. A religious symbol is not the creation of a subjective desire or work. If the symbol loses its

Boozer:
A symbol possesses a necessary character. It cannot be exchanged. On the other hand a sign is impotent in itself and can be exchanged at will. . . . The religious symbol is not the creation of a subjective desire or work. If the symbol loses its

ontological grounding, it declines and becomes a mere "thing," a sign impotent in itself. "Genuine symbols are not interchangeable at all and real symbols provide no objective knowledge, but yet a true awareness." The criterion of a symbol is that through it the unconditioned is clearly grasped in its unconditionedness.

Correlation as the correspondence of data means in this particular case that there is correspondence between religious symbols and that reality which these symbolize. Once a true religious symbol is discovered one can be sure that here is an implicit indication of the nature of God. (pp. 22-24)

ontological grounding, it declines and becomes a mere "thing," a sign impotent in itself. "Genuine symbols are not interchangeable at all and real symbols provide no objective knowledge, but yet a true awareness." The criterion of a symbol is that through it the unconditioned is clearly grasped in its unconditionedness. . . . (p. 125)

Correlation as the correspondence of data means in this particular case that there is correspondence between religious symbols and that reality which these symbolize. Once a true religious symbol has been discovered one can be sure that here is an implicit indication of the nature of God. (p. 267)

This last example is particularly revealing, because it shows not only the extent of King's plagiarism (every word on page 23 of King's text is lifted from Boozer), but also King's tactic of pasting together disparate sections of Boozer's text, in this case sections that are more than one hundred pages apart. The smooth and impressive manner in which King conjoined, word for word, different sections of Boozer's dissertation could not have been done without great circumspection and forethought.

The citations of such parallels could go on for many pages. King on freedom, page 312, is taken from pages 62 and 63 of Boozer. King on the "real interdependence of things and events," pages 25 and 26, is taken from page 269 of Boozer. King on the omnipresence of God, page 292, is taken from page 197 of Boozer. King on naturalism, or "humanism," page 18, is taken from pages 262 and 263 of Boozer. Et cetera.

As any devotee of detective stories well knows, it is the slight slips and blunders that most often carry the gravest consequence for the perpetrator of the crime. It is the dropped cuff link or forgotten matchbook that often reveals the perpetrator's identity and seals his fate, and King and his dissertation are no exceptions. King's forgotten matchbook and dropped cuff link are a comma and a typo.

Amid a discussion of Tillich's conception of "creation," we find the following parallel.

King:
But Tillich does not mean by creation an event which took place "once upon a time." Creation does not refer to an event, it rather indicates a condition, a relationship between God and the world. "It is the correlate to the analysis of man's *finitude, it* answers the question implied in man's finitude and infinitude [*sic*] generally." Man asks a question which, in existence, he cannot answer. But the question is answered by man's

Boozer:
But Tillich does not mean by creation an event which took place "once upon a time." Creation does not describe an event, it rather indicates a condition, a relationship between God and the world. "It is the correlate to the analysis of man's *finitude, it* answers the question implied in man's finitude and in finitude generally." Man asks a question which, in existence, he cannot answer. But the question is answered by man's

essential nature, his unity
with God. Creation is the
word given to the process
which actualizes man in
existence. To indicate the
gap between his essential
nature and his existential
nature man speaks of
creation. (p. 125)

essential nature, his unity
with God. Creation is the
word given to the process
which actualizes man in
existence. To indicate the
gap between his essential
nature and his existential
nature man speaks of
"creation." (pp. 45-46)

King has not only lifted this entire passage from Boozer's text, but he has even copied an error in punctuation. The grammatically incorrect comma between the two words I have italicized in both paragraphs does not appear in the text of Tillich, who correctly punctuated with a period. Boozer, in quoting these lines from page 252 of volume one of Tillich's *Systematic Theology*, mistakenly copied the period as a comma, and King simply copied Boozer's mistake.

More problems arise in the pages concluding King's section on Tillich. On page 159, King states that both he and the reader have now come to a question that has been "cropping up throughout our discussion of Tillich's God-concept, viz., the question of whether Tillich holds to an absolute quantitative monism." The reader can feel the buildup to King's exposition of his thesis, the pivotal point to which his previous 150 pages have been leading. Not surprisingly, this just happens to be one of the crucial questions to which Boozer also builds. As Boozer states on page 60, "We come now to a crucial issue for an understanding of Tillich. Is man a part of God in an absolute quantitative monism?" Virtually every line of King's concluding remarks on pages 159 and 160 can be found on pages 60 through 63 of Boozer's dissertation.

King:
Perhaps Tillich's most
explicit statement of
monism is his contention
that "man's love of
God is the love with

Boozer:
But perhaps the most
convincing statement of
monism is in terms of
love, that "man's love of
God is the love with

which God loves
himself. . . . The divine
life is the divine
self-love." . . . Passages
such as these cited
indicate an absolute
monism. . . . Tillich
affirms that there would
be no history unless man
were to some degree free;
that is, to some extent,
independent from God.
. . . He [man] is to some
extent "outside" the
divine life. This means
that he stands "in
actualized freedom, in an
existence which is no
longer united with
essence." (p. 160)

which God loves
himself. . . . The divine
life is the divine
self-love." . . . Passages
such as these certainly
indicate an absolute
monism. . . . There
would be no
history unless man
were to some degree free;
that is, to some degree
independent from God.
. . . He [man] is to some
extent "outside" the
divine life. "To be outside the
divine life means to stand in
actualized freedom, in an
existence which is no
longer united with
essence." (pp. 62-63)

King couldn't even resist Boozer's concluding comparisons. Boozer, page 61: "The similarity of Tillich's theology with Hegel's philosophy of spirit and Plotinus' philosophy of the One inclines one to interpret Tillich as an absolute monist." King, pages 159-160: "The similarity of Tillich's view at this point to Hegel's philosophy of spirit and Plotinus' philosophy of the One inclines one to interpret Tillich as an absolute monist."

It is amid these concluding remarks that King commits another error. King quotes the following from Tillich on page 159 of his thesis: "God is infinite because he has the finite within himself united with his infinity." Boozer uses this same quotation on page 61 of his thesis. Boozer, however, mistakenly credits it to page 282 of volume one of Tillich's *Systematic Theology*, whereas the correct page number is 252. King again copies Boozer's mistake and also types page 282 for his footnote to this quote. Interestingly enough, Boozer's next line in this paragraph is another quotation from page 252 of

Tillich's text—"The divine life is creative, actualizing itself in inexhaustible abundance." Not surprisingly, King follows with the same quote. This time, however, Boozer correctly cites page 252 in his footnote. King, still following Boozer's previous mistake, continues incorrectly to cite page 282.

No further evidence is needed to conclude that King plagiarized his doctoral dissertation. But many questions remain, such as how Professor L. Harold DeWolf, the first reader of both Boozer's and King's dissertations, could have overlooked—intentionally or unintentionally—the similarities between the two theses. And what are we to make of the disingenuous statements made by the editors of the King papers, whose reputations—by their own admission—are on the line? The idea that they needed nine months to review the evidence is absurd. A few hours with each text is all that is necessary.

The story of King's plagiarism has been suppressed for one simple reason: fear—fear of the massive retaliation that will be visited upon anyone who attempts to set the historical record straight, not just on King and his dissertation but on any historical incident on which the powers that be have declared an official position. Perhaps the editors of this magazine would have been wiser had they ignored this entire matter. But evidence of a cover-up made up our minds. We have learned, for example, that high-level administrators at several major universities have attempted to suppress this story and that at least one scholar has been bullied into silence. We also wonder why the National Endowment for the Humanities, which funds the King Papers Project and is well aware of the charge of plagiarism, has yet to take any action.

But other academic issues are also at stake. If one can believe the stories, plagiarism is on the rise in American universities. The most noted victim of plagiarism, Stephen Nissenbaum, has remarked (*Chronicle of Higher Education*, March 28, 1990) both upon the frequency of the crime and upon the academy's refusal to do anything about it for fear of getting involved or appearing to pass judgment. As he concludes, "To be willing to pass judgment is to protect everybody—not only those who are victimized by plagiarism, but also those who are falsely accused of it."

Then there is the reproof administered by the "ad interim" president of Boston University (see the Polemics & Exchanges section of this issue). Mr. Westling insists that scholars have "scrupulously examined and re-examined" King's dissertation without being able to identify "a single instance of plagiarism"—no "misattributed quotations," no "misleading paraphrases," and no "thoughts borrowed without due scholarly reference." He concludes his letter with this challenge: "If you or anyone else have evidence to the contrary, it should be presented." We issue a similar challenge to Mr. Westling, the editors of the King papers, and all other interested scholars: if you have any genuine evidence that might exonerate King, it should be presented.

A final comment. In their introduction to *We Shall Overcome: Martin Luther King, Jr., and the Black Freedom Struggle*, editors Peter Albert and Ronald Hoffman argue that King's legend has actually impeded the progress of civil rights in the United States. By lionizing the man, the movement has lost sight of the actual grassroots work on which success depends. This, of course, is nothing different from what Martin Luther King's best friend, the late Reverend Ralph Abernathy, had been saying all along: that the best thing King's supporters could do for themselves, for the movement, and for King is to celebrate the leader's virtues, his talents, his dreams, but not to make him into something he never was and something no man could ever be.

HISTORICAL UPDATE

Following *Chronicles'* denunciation of King's plagiarism in mid-August (Perspective, September 1990), the *Wall Street Journal* broke the story on November 9, after we had already put together the January issue. The *New York Times* then followed with its own version of the story on November 10. The editors of King's papers apparently believed the cover-up had continued for long enough.

In fact, Mr. Clayborne Carson now admits that he and some twenty other members and associates of his advisory board have known about the plagiarism for over three years, but chose to suppress the story until now. Actually Carson spoke not of "plagiarism," but of "a pattern of textual appropriation." Carson even instructed his staff members not to use "the p-word," and it may have been Carson's game of semantics that led the *Journal of American History* last June to reject his article discussing King's dissertation; as the *New York Times* reported, "the journal criticized Mr. Carson's unwillingness to take a firm stand on the question of plagiarism." Carson, it will be recalled, told the London *Telegraph* in September 1989, "It's really not true [that the dissertation was plagiarized]."

Boston University's ad interim president continued to claim until the eleventh hour, as is evidenced in his October 5 letter to *Chronicles* published on page four, that the dissertation had been "scrupulously examined" and that there was "not a single instance of plagiarism." Now, after the breaking of the story, Mr. Westling reports that the issue of plagiarism merits "close scrutiny." Apparently "scrupulously examined" means something less than "close scrutiny."

Most interesting is the spin that Mr. Carson and King's apologists are putting on the facts. Mr. Carson told the *Times* that King "acted unintentionally," and Joseph Lowery, president of the Southern Christian Leadership Conference, said King merely "overlooked some footnotes." The most ingenious excuse floated by King's apologists was that somehow King mistook the academy for a pulpit and wrote his dissertation the way black preachers, by their own admission, have long written their sermons: by plagiarizing. Keith Miller, a professor of rhetoric and composition at Arizona State University, has written two academic articles and is preparing a book on the many other papers and speeches that King also plagiarized. Apparently stealing words for a speech doesn't constitute plagiarism, or even "textual appropriation." Professor Miller and others call it "voice merging."

Serious questions of academic and journalistic integrity remain as a result of the attempted cover-up. First, Clayborne Carson has consistently misrepresented the facts of the case and continues, even after having admitted the plagiarism, to distort the evidence. Mr. Luker of Emory University, the associate editor of the papers, told the *Wall Street Journal* that, in dealing with King's plagiarism, "Clayborne has to achieve a position that is politically viable in the black community, politically respectable." No statement better shows the extent to which the editors of King's papers have ceased to act as scholars and begun to think like politicians. Carson receives public funds via the National Endowment for the Humanities for his abilities as a scholar, not as a politician or a civil rights leader, and as a result of suppressing this story the publication of King's works is now 16 months behind schedule. Carson has clearly forfeited his right to be taken seriously as an editor, and if he hasn't already resigned his position, he should do so immediately if only to restore some credibility to the project.

Second, David Garrow, a member of the project's advisory board and author of the Pulitzer Prize-winning biography of King, *Bearing the Cross*, also now admits to having known about King's plagiarism and deliberately suppressing the story. Shouldn't he give back his Pulitzer?

Third, if Jon Westling as ad interim president of Boston University was acting under his own initiative in concocting the story of King's innocence, then he is either incompetent or a liar. In either case, he should resign from the university he has disgraced. If he was acting as an agent for President John Silber, then the next move is up to Silber—who could, at the very least, strip King of his degree.

Fourth, the National Endowment for the Humanities has known about the plagiarism for over a year. Instead of coming clean with the American taxpayers, who have funded the King papers project with a reported half-million dollars, the Endowment simply sat on the facts. Mrs. Cheney owes us a full explanation of the role she and the NEH played in this matter.

Finally, the time has come for a frank and open debate on the significance of the King legacy. Unfortunately, the evidence is locked up in sealed FBI files. Instead of subjecting the nation to an unending series of disclosures and scandals, the government should unseal the documents. The issue is integrity—not of Martin Luther King, but of an American regime that refuses to tell the truth.

FIVE

"To Their Dismay, King Scholars Find a Troubling Pattern—Civil Rights Leader Was Lax in Attributing Some Parts of His Academic Papers" by Peter Waldman

The following was the Wall Street Journal's *principal coverage of the story. It ran as a front-page article on November 9, 1990, and is reprinted here with permission.*

Six years before his death, the Reverend Martin Luther King Jr. donated a large collection of his papers to Boston University. But the rest of his writings remained in his private study in Atlanta and scattered in church basements and file cabinets from coast to coast.

In 1984, Mr. King's widow, Coretta Scott King, founded the Martin Luther King Jr. Papers Project to collect the papers and produce a multi-volume collection. And she chose Clayborne Carson, a Stanford University historian, to lead the project.

Now, Mr. Carson, and his fellow researchers at Stanford, admirers of Mr. King, have found something they wish they had never discovered. They say that during his seven years of graduate school, Mr. King borrowed words and ideas extensively from other sources for his doctoral dissertation and other scholarly writings without giving proper citations.

"Several of King's academic papers, as well as his dissertation, contain numerous appropriated passages that can be defined as plagiarism," says Mr. Carson, senior editor and director of the project.

For instance, in parts of Mr. King's doctoral dissertation at Boston University, he used the same general structure, many of the same words and the same section titles as another doctoral dissertation written a few years earlier at the university. Though Mr. King paid tribute to his predecessor's work on the fifth page of his dissertation and cited it again in his bibliography, he footnoted the heavily borrowed text just twice in the course of the 343-page dissertation.

The project's discoveries have stirred debate, anguish and soul-searching among scholars who have worked on the project. They have kept the findings secret for nearly three years. Several student-researchers wondered why the information should be probed. Some resigned. One summer intern broke down in tears when she found out. Megan Maxwell, who joined the project as a Stanford under-graduate and became assistant archivist after graduation, says her initial reaction was anger, "a combination of 'Why didn't anyone catch him?' and 'Why didn't he know better?'"

Associate Editor Ralph Luker, a follower of Mr. King who was jailed during a civil rights protest, says he suffered "deep anxieties" over it and "many hours of lost sleep."

Seeing the extent of Mr. King's borrowings "had a tremendously shaking, emotional impact on me," says David Garrow, a member of the project's advisory board and author of "Bearing the Cross," a Pulitzer Prize-winning biography of Mr. King. "To me, 98 percent of what makes it most interesting is: Why did he do it? Was he so insecure that he thought this was the only way to get by? It's disconcerting, because it is fundamentally, phenomenally out of character with my entire sense of the man."

Mr. King's school papers comprise his most obscure and insignificant writings. They tended to explore esoteric themes within theology and had little to do with his ability to electrify the nation as a Baptist preacher and civil rights leader with his eloquent pleas for racial justice. In 1964, he was awarded the Nobel Peace Prize, and in 1984 Congress declared his birthday a federal holiday.

The discovery is part of a revisionist picture of Mr. King that has been emerging from recent books and academic papers. Those point up some of his human flaws and portray him as less of a myth and more of a man, as more of a brilliant leader than a ground-breaking thinker. Perhaps the most controversial was Ralph Abernathy's recent autobiography, which includes allegations that Mr. King spent time with a woman friend the last night of his life.

A book due out next spring will examine the origins of many of Mr. King's speeches, sermons and essays. Author Keith Miller, a professor of rhetoric and composition at Arizona State University, won't comment on his research. But in two academic articles published in 1986 and last January, Mr. Miller shows how passages in Mr. King's books *Strength to Love* and *Stride Toward Freedom* and in his famous essay "Letter From Birmingham City Jail" echoed parts of sermons and books by several ministers and writers, particularly Harry Emerson Fosdick, who was at Riverside Church in New York, and Harris Wofford, author of a book on nonviolence and now Pennsylvania's labor secretary.

For example, Mr. Miller points out, Mr. King echoed Mr. Fosdick nearly word-for-word when he wrote: "Any religion that professes to be concerned about the souls of men and is not concerned about the slums that damn them . . . is a spiritually moribund religion."

Mr. Miller believes Mr. King's technique stemmed from the oral traditions of the black church. There, words weren't regarded as private property but as a shared resource for the community. He and others believe Mr. King excelled at "voice merging," as scholars call it, blending other people's words with his own.

From 1948 to 1955, Mr. King received high marks as a divinity student at Crozer Theological Seminary in Pennsylvania, where he graduated at the top of his class, and then as a doctoral candidate at Boston University. The questions about his academic work surfaced in late 1987, nearly 20 years after his death. A Stanford graduate student working for the King Papers Project found that, in some parts of Mr. King's dissertation, he lifted passages nearly word-for-word from other texts without using any quotation marks or footnotes.

In other places in his dissertation, titled "A Comparison of the Conceptions of God in the Thinking of Paul Tillich and Henry Nelson Wieman," Mr. King used quotation marks and footnotes to mark part of a passage, but after the quotation marks ended, the borrowed text continued. Another project researcher discovered the similarities to the earlier dissertation.

After those issues surfaced, Mr. Carson asked his staff to check the sources of nearly all of Mr. King's academic work. A pattern emerged. Most of Mr. King's papers had many original thoughts. But throughout the seven years of graduate school, Mr. King's essays, particularly in his major field of graduate study, systematic theology, often borrowed without citing them in accordance with academic rules.

For the 46-year-old Mr. Carson, the discovery of Mr. King's questionable citation practices became an unwelcome obsession. Mr. Carson attended his first civil rights demonstration as a college freshman in 1963—the legendary March on Washington, where he heard Mr. King's "I Have a Dream" speech—and later was jailed for participating in a protest. As editor of the King papers, however, Mr. Carson has been determined "to keep a balance between the tendency to idealize and the tendency to debunk," he says. "My job is to explain, not to defend and not to attack."

The role has been an exasperating one. After the citation problems emerged, three project editors and a half-dozen student-researchers spent nearly two years annotating all of Mr. King's 150 or so academic papers. The long digression not only kept editors and students from doing more interesting research, but it threw the project's first volume, originally due out this January, 16 months behind schedule. The delay strained the finances of the project, funded mostly by the National Endowment for the Humanities and Stanford.

Mr. Carson tries not to be judgmental about the discoveries. He asked staff members to refrain from using the word "plagiarism" around the office, giving rise among the scholars to the euphemism "the p-word." But that doesn't prevent Mr. Carson and his fellow researchers from trying to figure out the central question: Why?

Mr. King's academic papers demonstrated that he had a working knowledge of the use of footnotes, bibliographies and other conventions. Records show that he took a thesis-writing class at Boston University in which the teacher lectured on proper methods of citation. Somewhere, in most of Mr. King's scholarly essays, he cited the sources from which he borrowed material, though those citations rarely indicated the extent of his appropriations.

It is doubtful that Mr. King intended to slip anything past his dissertation adviser, L. Harold DeWolf. Three years before Mr. King completed his dissertation, Mr. DeWolf had been the doctoral adviser for a student named Jack Boozer, author of the dissertation that Mr. King so heavily relied on in parts of his own. Mr. DeWolf's signature appeared on the approval pages of both dissertations. (Mr. Boozer died in 1989. His wife, Ruth, says he learned about the project's findings shortly before his death. "He told me he'd be so honored and so glad if there were anything that Martin Luther King could have used from his work," she says.)

Mr. Carson guesses that Mr. King didn't think he was doing anything wrong. "The best evidence for that," he says, "is that he saved his papers and donated them to an archive—at B.U. of all places."

Mr. King wrote much of his dissertation in 1954, after becoming pastor of Dexter Avenue Baptist Church in Montgomery, Alabama. He worked on the manuscript early in the morning and late at night, according to biographical accounts, while instituting a number of church programs and preaching at churches and colleges across the South. "It was possible that the press of his work caused him to be careless," suggests Cornish Rogers, a friend and classmate of Mr. King's at Boston University and now a professor at the School of Theology at Claremont, California.

Several researchers at the project have focused much of their disappointment on Mr. King's professors, who they say must have recognized the problems but didn't act. "Their assumption was they were training someone to go teach in a predominantly black college in the South," says Penny Russell, who worked for five years as administrator and associate editor of the project. "Were they setting up different standards?"

Mr. DeWolf, Mr. King's doctoral adviser, has died. S. Paul Schilling, the so-called second reader of Mr. King's dissertation at Boston University, has reviewed the project's findings. He says that Mr. King's dissertation was among the first he ever evaluated and that "I was not sufficiently perceptive in regard to plagiarism." Mr. Schilling did warn Mr. King in an early draft of the dissertation that he had "almost exactly quoted" another writer without using quotation marks, but Mr. King didn't make the suggested revisions. Mr. Schilling vehemently denies that he or Mr. DeWolf had any double standards.

All of this presented difficult issues to the project. Among them: How should the project reveal its findings? And should the project use footnotes in the volumes to note each borrowed passage? Not only would that dramatically increase the length of the books, but Mr. Carson worried about the visual impact of page after page of footnotes occupying as much or more space as Mr. King's own writing.

The issues were discussed in October 1989 at a meeting in Atlanta of the project's advisory board. Mrs. King presided. She opened the meeting with a prayer and thanked the dozen or so scholars for their attendance. For the rest of the all-day meeting, Mrs. King said almost nothing, registering little emotion on her face, according to people in attendance. Through a spokesman, she deferred inquiries for this article to Mr. Carson.

After several hours of sometimes emotional discussion, the advisory board agreed that Mr. Carson should do two things: Publish the academic papers with complete footnotes, regardless of the visual effect, and write a separate scholarly article, outlining and interpreting the citation problems.

In June, Mr. Carson submitted a paper on Mr. King's use of citations to the *Journal of American History*. It was rejected. Neither Mr. Carson nor the journal will discuss why. But project staff members say the journal criticized Mr. Carson's unwillingness to take a firm stand on the question of plagiarism.

Mr. Carson is revising the piece for resubmission. (Last week, when he learned the *Wall Street Journal* was preparing this article, he agreed to be interviewed.) If accepted, his article will probably appear in the *Journal of American History*'s June issue. Staff members say he is addressing the question of plagiarism more directly and may include a chart showing the approximate percentages in the dissertation of Mr. King's own words and the words of others. For now, Mr. Carson will say only that a "substantial" amount was borrowed.

Mr. Carson does not have an easy task. Says Mr. Luker, the associate editor, who is based at Emory University: "Clayborne has to achieve a position that is politically viable in the black community, politically respectable and acceptable in the academic community, and maintain a friendly relationship with Mrs. King."

SIX

"Embargoed"
by Charles Babington

Charles Babington's article in the January 28, 1991, issue of the New Republic *was the first article to expose the many publishers and editors who had long known about King's plagiarisms but refused to cover the story. It is reprinted here with permission.*

On November 9 the *Wall Street Journal* published what was widely seen as a solid, page-one scoop: Martin Luther King had plagiarized parts of his doctoral dissertation. The next day the rest of the press followed with front-page stories, crediting the *Journal* for the news. What they didn't reveal was that many of them had had the story themselves—a story that had been widely rumored, and easily available, for a year—and not printed it. The *Washington Post*, the *New York Times*, the *Atlanta Journal/Constitution*, and the *New Republic* had all failed to run articles even though at least one editor at each journal knew of the King story last spring, and three right-wing journals had already published it.

The story begins on December 3, 1989—eleven months before the *Wall Street Journal's* coup. The *Sunday Telegraph* of London carried an article headlined: "Martin Luther King—Was He a Plagiarist?" The column, by Frank Johnson under the pen name Mandrake, said, "Researchers in his native Georgia must soon decide whether to reveal that the late Dr. King . . . was—in addition to his other human failings—a plagiarist." The column even identified the smoking gun—the dissertation of fellow Boston University student Jack Boozer, from whom King lifted large passages verbatim. Mandrake quoted Ralph Luker of Atlanta, top assistant to Clayborne Carson, the Stanford historian chosen by Coretta Scott King to direct the King Papers Project. Luker virtually confirmed the allegations with his painstaking efforts to sidestep all questions about plagiarism. As a final goad, Mandrake wrote, "The story has not yet been published in the United States." Johnson says he got the King plagiarism story from a British professor who had visited the United States, and that he's not surprised the U.S. press ignored his article. "American reporters' powers of perception tend to fail them on questions of race, gender, gays," he told me.

Articles in the *Sunday Telegraph* (circulation 585,000) are available through Nexis, the computer database service used by many U.S. news organizations and businesses. Any reporter who heard the talk of King's plagiarism in early 1990 could have had Mandrake's road map in minutes by asking Nexis for articles containing the words "Martin Luther King" and "plagiarism." From there, a visit to Boston University's library—which contains both Boozer's and King's dissertations—would have provided the information for the story.

On January 22, 1990, *The Spotlight*, the Liberty Lobby's organ, which claims a circulation of 100,000, carried a front-page story: "King Stole PhD Thesis, According to Evidence." The article, next to an item on "QUEER legislation" and an ad for a $5 cassette on "Alcohol, the Devil's A Bomb," rehashed the Mandrake column. It also included its own interview with Luker, who again refused to confirm or deny the plagiarism charge.

From March 1 to 3 about fifty members of the Southern Intellectual History Circle met in Chapel Hill, North Carolina. "It was very clear that the story [of King's plagiarism] was in the academic cocktail-party gossip network by then," says Luker, who attended. One conferee was University of North Carolina sociologist John Shelton Reed, and he soon began drafting his monthly column for *Chronicles*, the magazine of the conservative Rockford Institute in Illinois. He cited the *Telegraph* story, and the gossip in American academia. So widespread is the talk, he continued, "I presume that by the time this letter sees print I won't be telling you anything you don't know."

But Reed balked at publishing. He was surprised the U.S. press still had not written about the plagiarism as his June publication date neared, and says he didn't care to see headlines saying, "Reed alleges King plagiarism." In his proposed column Reed called on B.U. to replace King's Ph.D. with an honorary doctorate. As a courtesy, he mailed a copy to the university's interim president, Jon Westling. Westling responded with "a stern letter" insisting that the allegations were totally false, Reed says. At the last minute Reed withdrew his column. (As late as October Westling wrote *Chronicles* saying King's "dissertation has, in fact, been scrupulously examined and reexamined by scholars. . . . Not a single instance of plagiarism of any sort has been identified.")

In September, peeved by his columnist's fickleness, *Chronicles* editor Thomas Fleming wrote an article saying, "King, it has been recently revealed, apparently plagiarized his Boston University doctoral dissertation." Meanwhile, *Chronicles* reporter Ted Pappas obtained copies of the King and Boozer dissertations, located extensive examples of King's filching, and laid them out in an article. It ran in January's issue, which, he says, "we had already put together" when the *Wall Street Journal* article appeared.

By mid-1990 Clayborne Carson realized that talk of the plagiarism—which he had known about since late 1987—was seeping out. He held a handful of reporters at bay by misleading them about the extent of the problem. Scholars and government officials, meanwhile, agreed to remain silent. In early 1990 Carson's team told its main underwriter, the National Endowment for the Humanities, of the plagiarism. (Lynne Cheney and fellow officials were not obligated to divulge the information, NEH spokesmen say. And they didn't.) The previous October Carson had described his discoveries to Mrs. King and the project's board of directors. They agreed he should include the findings in a scholarly article for the quarterly *Journal of American History*, to be published in December 1990. The *Journal*, however, rejected his first draft in a dispute over how to address the plagiarism matter. Carson and his colleagues began revising the piece for a mid-1991 issue. Meanwhile, word of the plagiarism was leaking from Atlanta-based scholars and former students who had worked on the King Papers Project team housed at Emory

University. That group, unlike Carson's Stanford-based contingent, had the Boozer dissertation, which is why press attention came to focus on the borrowing from Boozer. In fact, Carson says, King's greatest source of plagiarized material came from the theologian Paul Tillich.

The first U.S. reporter to approach Carson with questions about plagiarism was the *Washington Post*'s Dan Balz. Balz says he interviewed Carson last spring and received "a less alarmist view of what they had" about the plagiarism. Balz, unaware of the Mandrake column, knew nothing of Boozer. He says the *Post* did a database search, but asked for information about the King Papers Project rather than "King" and "plagiarism." Balz says Carson told him, "Once we've got all the evidence assembled, you can come out and look at it and draw your own conclusions." Balz agreed, after obtaining what he thought was Carson's promise to alert him if other reporters came snooping around. Through the summer and early fall, Carson kept telling Balz that his researchers needed more time. When I asked Carson if he had led Balz to believe there was less to the plagiarism story than there really was, he replied: "Definitely. I don't apologize for the fact I tried to play it down. . . . I wasn't about to break the story to someone who just asked" about King's plagiarism in general terms.

By autumn Carson got a call from Peter Waldman, the Atlanta-based *Wall Street Journal* reporter who eventually got the scoop. At first Carson did his usual stonewalling. "I told him the same thing— no big deal, don't call us, we'll call you," Carson says. But a few weeks later Waldman called him back to tell him he had the Boozer dissertation. According to Carson, Waldman said, "We'll go to press with or without you." Carson cooperated.

What had happened at the *Post*? Despite the paper's troubled relations with black readers, Balz and deputy managing editor Robert Kaiser say the paper didn't deliberately drag its feet on the King story. Kaiser says the paper exercised normal caution "because of the problem of besmirching people's reputations on the basis of hearsay." The *Post*'s ombudsman, Richard Harwood, agrees, but adds: "I suspect that we pursue more rapidly and vigorously things about some people than we do about other people."

The *Atlanta Journal/Constitution* has no one to blame but itself. Frances Schwartzkopff, a rookie suburban reporter, picked up the plagiarism rumor last spring from the same source that Waldman did—a former Emory student who had worked on the King editing project. Hesitating at first out of concern for the source, she says, "I told my editors after a month or so." That triggered a debate about who should handle the story, how to pursue it, etc. It's unclear exactly what happened, but the reporter finally assigned to the story knew nothing of Schwartzkopff's information (including the Boozer connection) and started reporting from scratch.

The *New York Times* was even more hapless. An editor for the paper's book review section learned of the King plagiarism from a prominent historian, who swore the editor to secrecy in early 1990. Rebecca Sinkler, editor of the *Times's Book Review*, says the paper has a strict policy of telling the news staff about newsworthy tips. "I certainly never heard diddly about this," she says. When I asked Anthony DePalma, the *Times* reporter who followed up the *Wall Street Journal's* scoop, about reports that a book review sub-editor had sat on the story, he said he'd heard the same story, and tried to learn the editor's identity, to no avail.

At the *New Republic*, literary editor Leon Wieseltier learned of the King plagiarism last spring from Eugene Genovese, a historian now living in Atlanta. "I thought it was a story that was going to stir people, and could easily be put to all sorts of unpleasant purposes," Wieseltier says. So the magazine's editors "decided early on—I think correctly, since this was a story about ideas and texts—that it would require a certain amount of scholarly skill" from the writer. The magazine approached several historians, all of whom took some time to consider, and decline, the assignment. But sentimentality and "correct politics" inhibited the editors from vigorously pursuing the story. In retrospect, says Martin Peretz, TNR's editor in chief, the magazine reacted too gingerly because of the story's racial overtones. "Everybody suddenly got palsied," he says.

Carson, who was less than forthcoming until the *Wall Street Journal* got the goods, can take some pride in his buying of time before the plagiarism story broke. "Looking back," he says, "it might have been naive to think it would wait for the scholarly process to work.

MARTIN LUTHER KING, JR.

But it almost worked."

SEVEN

Letter from Walter G. Muelder of Boston University to *Chronicles*

Walter G. Muelder, Dean Emeritus of Boston University's School of Theology, sent Chronicles *the following letter for publication in its April 1991 issue.*

The article by Theodore Pappas in the January 1991 issue of *Chronicles* suggests that Jon Westling of Boston University was either complicit in a cover-up or incompetent in the pursuit of the facts regarding the King plagiarism case. These charges are grossly unfair. I was the dean of the School of Theology when Martin Luther King, Jr., was pursuing doctoral studies in the Graduate School. L. Harold DeWolf and S. Paul Schilling were first and second readers respectively of King's dissertation. DeWolf is deceased and Schilling (retired in 1969) now lives in Maryland. DeWolf was also the major professor for Boozer, whose dissertation is cited in the recent article.

When ad interim president Westling received a communication from John Shelton Reed regarding a forthcoming article on King's dissertation, Westling contacted me for any information I might have about the alleged plagiarism. I had never heard of such a thing. I telephoned Professor Schilling on May 28. He assured me that DeWolf and he had read the dissertation with care and to his knowledge this kind of accusation had never been raised. (Schilling was not on the faculty when Boozer wrote his dissertation.) I advised Jon Westling of my conversation with Schilling. Also, I suggested that the Center for King Studies in Atlanta might appropriately be informed of the allegations.

Jon Westling directed the University's legal counsel to inform Mrs. King's counsel about the allegations. At or about that time Westling got in touch with Clayborne Carson at Stanford and the latter unambiguously denied that there was any plagiarism in King's dissertation. Reed was so informed. The upshot of all these efforts was that no evidence by anyone—not by Reed, or Carson, or Schilling, or Mrs. King—supported the allegations so far as President Westling or I knew. It was on the basis of this lack of evidence that Jon Westling wrote his letter to *Chronicles*.

Whatever evidence has been forthcoming since last May is a matter to be dealt with on its own merits, but the ad interim president of Boston University has in no way been involved in any "cover-up" or "incompetence" or falsification of history. In fact, as soon as the story broke in the *Wall Street Journal* this fall, he acted promptly in setting up a committee of investigation. In May both Westling and I believed that the rumor of plagiarism had been laid to rest as just that. Like others, we were startled to learn that quite another scenario of facts and accusations had been evolving all along. I trust that this correction of the article in *Chronicles* will clarify Jon Westling's actual relation to the unfinished business of the King plagiarism case.

EIGHT

Editorial response to Mr. Muelder and update to the story
by Theodore Pappas

This editorial ran in the same April 1991 issue of Chronicles *in which Mr. Muelder's letter appeared.*

The story of Martin Luther King, Jr.'s plagiarism has elicited a number of responses, most of them disingenuous. Walter Muelder, the former dean of Boston University's School of Theology, would like to exculpate Boston University's Jon Westling (see page four of the April issue) but only succeeds in making matters worse. Mr. Muelder casually reveals what should have been evident all along: that from beginning to end, from the December 1989 interview with the London *Telegraph* to the present, King Papers editor Clayborne Carson has consistently misrepresented the facts and distorted the evidence. According to Mr. Muelder, Mr. Carson denied King's plagiarism to Mr. Westling "unambiguously," and apparently this is where the latter got the notion that "not a single instance" of plagiarism is evident in any of the 343 pages of King's dissertation. One scholar who did not hesitate to use the "p-word" was King's biographer, David Garrow. Misled by the *New York Times'* November 10 story, we accused Mr. Garrow of being part of the cover-up. We were mistaken and apologize. Mr. Garrow apparently found out the story about the same time as other King scholars and had been assured that Mr. Carson would be forthcoming with the truth.

In fact, even though it is now known that King plagiarized far more than just his doctoral dissertation, including many of his other essays and speeches, Mr. Carson continues his campaign of deception and distortion. An article in the November/December 1990 *Stanford Observer* quotes him as saying "his [King's] professors did not expect originality in his compositions." Surely *Dr.* Carson, Ph.D., knows that the chief requirement of a doctoral dissertation is that it constitute an *original* contribution to scholarship. But the prize for duplicity goes to the *Stanford Observer* itself, which entitled its unsigned article "Allegation of Plagiarism." Even Carson has quit using the word "allegation."

Mr. Carson laid on another coat of whitewash in a January 16 article in the *Chronicle of Higher Education.* In a tangle of half-truths and misrepresentations, Mr. Carson comes to the nub of the matter: "His legitimate utilization of political, philosophical, and literary texts—particularly those expressing the nation's democratic ideals— inspired and mobilized many Americans, thereby advancing the cause of social justice." Translation: plagiarism is excusable if done for the furtherance of "politically correct" causes. Having settled the ethical question for us, Mr. Carson then says we are to admire "King as the pre-eminent American orator of the 20th century," even while "recognizing that textual appropriation was one aspect of a successful composition method." It has always been realized that orators and scholars do their work in a tradition in which ideas and expressions can become common property, but what would we think of Burke or Lincoln if they had systematically attempted to pass off the work of others as their own? The answer is clear: we would classify them with the likes of a Joe Biden—or a Martin Luther King.

Mr. Muelder's letter also clarifies something about Jon Westling of Boston University: it reveals the seriousness with which Mr. Westling viewed this matter. After John Reed's letter, Mr. Westling contacted Mr. Muelder and had the latter contact Mr. S. Paul Schilling of Maryland, the second reader of King's dissertation. Mr. Westling then contacted Mrs. King and the Center for King Studies in Atlanta and Clayborne Carson of Stanford, wrote John Reed in North Carolina, and even felt the need to address the "false story" of King's plagiarism, which by his own admission was spreading "like whooping cough among the unvaccinated," by writing *Chronicles* the now infamous October 5 letter. Mr. Westling obviously ran up a lot of phone bills and used a lot of stamps.

Why, then, if Mr. Westling so clearly understood the seriousness of this matter and the serious repercussions that such a story could have for the reputation of the university he represents, did he rely exclusively on information from outside sources, some of which would have an obvious interest in seeing such a charge denied and such a story suppressed? Why, in other words, did he do everything but the simplest and most logical and conclusive action of all, that of picking up the theses and examining the evidence for himself? Or why, at the very least, did he not have an aide, or his theology department, do it for him? After all, he and Boston University were in the best position of anyone to either deny or substantiate the validity of the charge. Boston University is the only university in the world that has both King's and Boozer's dissertations.

Mr. Westling has floated a number of excuses to justify his actions. His plea to the *Chicago Tribune* was that "I'm just an academic administrator trying to keep the story straight." Westling apparently is even trying to discredit *Chronicles* by telling people that we sat on the evidence and deliberately delayed our story all in an effort to make him look bad. In fact, we received a copy of Boozer's dissertation a mere two weeks before Mr. Westling sent us his letter, and we received Boozer's actual dissertation from Boston University's Interlibrary Loan Department only four days before; his own library would be happy to substantiate this fact. A first draft of my article was completed within two weeks of receiving the evidence, which then began the two-month publishing process through which all *Chronicles* articles must pass.

Boston University had the opportunity to control the cards in this matter, but Mr. Westling gave away the game. By placing his and his university's reputation in the hands of Clayborne Carson and his coterie at the King Papers Project, Mr. Westling earned the academic dunce cap awarded to him by James Warren of the *Chicago Tribune*.

As we now know, a number of major newspapers knew the facts of this story but deliberately refused to publish them. According to Charles Babington's January 28, 1991, article in the *New Republic*, the *Washington Post*, the *New York Times*, the *Atlanta Journal/Constitution*, and the *New Republic* had all refused to run articles though at least one editor at each publication knew of this story as far back as last spring. The backpedalling of the *Wall Street Journal* has been particularly entertaining: the *Journal* reported the plagiarism on November 9, ran a November 15 editorial that says King's plagiarisms don't reflect on the character of Mr. King but rather "tell something about the rest of us," and then published a January 21 editorial by a Professor George McLean that praises King's plagiarized dissertation as "a contribution in scholarship for which his doctorate was richly deserved."

The way in which the *Journal* reported this story did not go unnoticed by the London *Telegraph*, which wrote: "such is the cravenness of the U.S. media when it comes to race that no newspaper followed [our December 1989] story, until Friday. Then, in an article full of apologetic, mealy-mouthed phrases, the *Wall Street Journal* confirmed our findings." But perhaps the *Journal*'s cravenness shouldn't have surprised us. After all, the *Journal* tipped its hand in its November 15 editorial, when it stressed the importance of covering this story in a "carefully modulated" way.

Last September we received an interesting call from a man who described himself as a black college professor. He called in response to Thomas Fleming's September Perspective, the essay in which the charges against King were mentioned and which engendered the October 5 letter from Jon Westling. Our caller said two things. First, that if we had evidence that King was indeed a plagiarist, then we should publish it forthwith, which we assured him we were in the process of doing. Second, he stated that if the charges proved to be true, then he would propose to his colleagues that the name of the hall his college had named in honor of Mr. King be immediately changed. Lecturing about academic standards in "Martin Luther King Hall" would be the height of hypocrisy and an insult to his college, he said.

Such painful honesty is apparently beyond the capacity of most academics, administrators, and American journalists.

NINE

Editorial update to the story
by Theodore Pappas

The following editorial on the continuing ramifications of King's plagiarisms appeared in the June 1991 issue of Chronicles.

Martin Luther King's plagiarism continues to send after-shocks. Ralph Luker has been dropped as the associate editor of the King Papers Project; his contract was not renewed last January. Clayborne Carson's staff has reportedly been in disarray for quite some time, and sources associated with the project called Luker "expendable," the "fall guy," the "sacrificial lamb" needed to get the King Papers Project back on track. It was Luker's misfortune to be editing the project's volume that dealt with King's plagiarized dissertation.

Sources also cite Coretta King as being "less than helpful" throughout this entire episode. Her refusal to release her husband's handwritten dissertation note cards reportedly strained her relations with Carson and the project, and one source even blamed her uncooperativeness for the project's delay in coming forth with the evidence of King's plagiarism. Such excuses won't wash. Mrs. King may be as guilty as Mr. Carson is in hindering the uncovering of the truth, and note cards may be helpful in explaining how the plagiarism was conducted, but neither Mrs. King's cooperation nor the dissertation note cards are needed to substantiate King's offense.

One source attempted to defend the project's handling of this matter by arguing, "It's not the business of scholars to report politically sensitive information, that's the business of journalists." Recent history, however, doesn't bear this out. Innumerable scholars were involved in compiling the Kurt Waldheim dossier, and their discoveries were published as soon as they were made. Nor did the editors at the University of Nebraska Press lie about the evidence, misrepresent the facts, or attempt a cover-up of the issue—as Clayborne Carson has admittedly done—when they came upon the pro-fascist writings of Paul de Man. The scholarly community did its job in both instances: it pursued the truth and set forth the evidence for the world to see and examine for itself.

In fact, the University of Nebraska Press started editing De Man's writings about the same time Clayborne Carson claims to have uncovered solid evidence of King's plagiarism, in late 1987, and since then Nebraska has published two formidable books on De Man. What has Clayborne Carson accomplished during this same time? He has received a reported half-million dollars of the taxpayers' money and published not a single volume of King's works—and the King Papers Project has been in existence for seven years. The one article he did write on the subject was rejected by the *Journal of American History* because of his lack of forthrightness with the evidence; as one source put it, Carson was asked to rewrite the article "with more of an interpretation." The *Journal* has scheduled a round-table discussion of King's plagiarism for its spring issue.

President John Silber of Boston University has meanwhile asked Robert Neville, the dean of B.U.'s School of Theology, to head a four-person committee to "investigate" King's plagiarism. Mr. Neville told me that the committee had completed its investigation and passed on its findings to Silber, who as of this writing had not yet commented publicly on the committee's report. Let's hope the committee concentrated on what action B.U. should take in light of King's plagiarism instead of stonewalling with an "investigation" into the "allegation" of plagiarism. Establishing a committee to investigate the validity of the charge is what Jon Westling and B.U. should have done eight months ago. Establishing a committee to do so now is about as useful as investigating whether John Silber really isn't governor of Massachusetts.

Finally, in a matter not entirely unrelated, Arizonans were indeed punished for their politically incorrect vote on a paid holiday to honor King. Paul Tagliabue, the Torquemada of professional football, announced the sentence at the NFL owners' annual *auto-da-fé* last March: the 1993 Super Bowl would be moved from Phoenix to either San Diego or Pasadena. Tagliabue hinted that, if Arizonans would recant their heathen ways by voting in a paid holiday for King next year, the NFL might grace Phoenix with the Super Bowl in 1996.

To anyone who believes voting costs nothing in America—think again.

TEN

"A Houdini of Time"
by Theodore Pappas

This review of Clayborne Carson's The Papers of Martin Luther King, Jr. Volume I: Called to Serve, January 1929-June 1951 *(University of California Press, 1992) and of Keith Miller's* Voice of Deliverance: The Language of Martin Luther King, Jr. and Its Sources *(The Free Press, 1992) appeared in the November 1992 issue of* Chronicles.

After seven years on public and private payrolls as senior editor of the King Papers Project, Clayborne Carson has finally produced the first volume of MLK's papers. The project began in 1984, and since 1986 has received a half-million dollars of the taxpayers' money via the National Endowment for the Humanities. Concerning the amount of *public* funds going directly to Carson's salary, the NEH says "this is confidential information off-limits to the *public*." The project is also backed by the National Historical Publications and Records Commission, James Irvine Foundation, Ford Foundation, Rockefeller Foundation, Stanford University, Emory University, IBM, Intel, and the Stanford University Associates of the King Papers Project. These are many of the same sources that, along with the NEH, have supported the Marcus Garvey and Universal Negro Improvement Association Papers, whose U.C.L.A. editor began collecting documents in 1970 and has still finished only seven volumes of the 11-volume set. Clyde Wilson, editor of the Papers of John C. Calhoun, has—with a staff of one and a bare-bones budget—published 11 volumes in 15 years.

If Clayborne Carson had been candid with the public from the very beginning of the controversy over King's plagiarisms the long delay in publishing the first volume might be excused and justified. After all, the thousands of plagiarized passages in King's sermons, speeches, college papers, seminary essays, doctoral dissertation, and published book reviews and articles could so overwhelm an editor that a plea for patience might be understandable. But Carson chose duplicity over disclosure, opting to misrepresent the facts, to hide the truth as long as possible, and to set in motion the official spin on the controversy.

In 1989, when he was asked by Frank Johnson of the London *Telegraph* about the "rumor" that King plagiarized his 1955 doctoral dissertation, Carson called the charge unwarranted, saying "It's really not true [that King plagiarized]." Even after the story broke Carson persisted in applying whitewash with half-truths and academic double-talk. He spoke not of plagiarism—the dreaded "p-word" that he forbade everyone at the project's headquarters at Stanford ever to use—but of "paraphrasing," "similarities," and "textual appropriations" as "part of a successful composition method." This blather and "lack of forthrightness" with the truth led the *Journal of American History* to reject the article he had submitted to explain the controversy.

But the whitewash went well beyond Carson and the King Papers Project. Boston University's then acting president, Jon Westling, flatly denied in *Chronicles* that "a single instance of plagiarism of any sort has been identified," and B.U.'s "Martin Luther King Professor of Social Ethics," John Cartwright, who even sat on the B.U. committee that analyzed King's thesis, claimed "there is no obvious indication in the dissertation that he inappropriately utilized material." The *Wall Street Journal* admitted King's plagiarism, but then concluded that the theft does not reflect on his character but rather "tells something about the rest of us." Such sophistry and drivel did not get past the London *Telegraph*, which reported "such is the cravenness of the U.S. media when it comes to race that no newspaper followed [our 1989] story. . . . Then, in an article full of apologetic, mealy-mouthed phrases, the *Wall Street Journal* confirmed our findings."

Not surprisingly, Carson and the project have come out of the controversy nearly as clean and unscathed as King has himself. The *Washington Post* recently hailed Carson's work in an article entitled "Called to Serve," and Eugene Genovese in a review of volume one for the *New Republic* wrote glowingly of Carson's "professional integrity," his "tact and good sense," and of the "splendid job" of volume editor Ralph Luker, declaring that Coretta King and her advisory board have "every reason to be proud of their choice of a general editor and of the staff he put together." Amid encomia and hagiography as heavy as this, it seems heartless to point out that Ralph Luker was long ago fired from the King Papers Project as the "fall guy" for the controversy over King's dissertation, that Coretta King and Carson locked horns in a bitter struggle over control of King's dissertation note cards, and that one of Carson's associates blames the publication delays and problems with the project on Coretta King's lack of cooperation.

Volume one documents the period from King's birth to his application to the doctoral program at B.U. and summarizes his family history in an introduction by the volume editors. King was born in Atlanta, Georgia, in 1929, the son of the revered pastor of Ebenezer Baptist Church. After attending a number of schools in Atlanta, he passed a special examination in 1944 to enter Morehouse College without having earned his high school diploma. He graduated in 1948 with a degree in sociology and entered the Crozer Theological Seminary in Chester, Pennsylvania. Obtaining his bachelor's degree in divinity in 1951, he then enrolled in the doctoral program at B.U.'s School of Theology.

King was reared, in his own words, "in a very congenial home situation," with parents who "always lived together very intimately." Closest to him was his maternal grandmother, whose death in 1941 left him emotionally unstable. Remorseful because he had learned of her fatal heart attack while attending a parade without his parents' permission, the 12-year-old Martin attempted suicide by jumping from a second-story window.

Most striking about the Kings is the affluence they enjoyed during the Depression. As King, Sr., himself admitted, "the deacons took great pride in knowing that [he] was the best-paid Negro minister in the city." In fact, while millions of white and black Americans were queuing in bread lines, King, Sr., was touring France, Italy, Germany, and the Holy Land. Though he refused to join the migration to the more prestigious areas of Atlanta to which middle- and upper-middle-class blacks like himself were then moving, King's father did buy a larger home in his same neighborhood, "thus fulfilling a childhood ambition of King, Sr., to own such a house. Enjoying the benefits of his family's affluence, King, Jr., became active in the social life of middle-class Atlanta."

The key phrase above reads not "middle-class *black* Atlanta" but simply "middle-class Atlanta," and it was the bourgeois culture of white America that shaped King's early adult years. When King entered the Crozer Theological Seminary in 1948, he was one of only 11 black students of a student body nearing a hundred. He immersed himself "in the social and intellectual life of a predominantly white, northern seminary," and "most accounts of King's experiences at Crozer suggest that he actively sought out social contacts with white students and faculty members." Known for his wonderful oratorical skills, King became one of the most popular students on campus and was even elected president of the student body, a feat that did not go unnoticed among the faculty and administration. As Crozer's Professor Morton Enslin wrote in his letter of recommendation for King to B.U.,

> The fact that with our student body largely Southern in constitution a colored man should be elected to and be popular [in] such a position is in itself no mean recommendation. The comparatively small number of forward-looking and thoroughly trained negro leaders is, as I am sure you will agree, still so small that it is more than an even chance that one as adequately trained as King will find ample opportunity for useful service. He is entirely free from those somewhat annoying qualities which some men of his race acquire when they find themselves in the distinct higher percent of their group.

King's eagerness and ability to mix well with white students becomes significant when seen in light of his performance during Crozer's fieldwork program. On the basis of King's preaching to black congregations, the evaluator of the program, the Reverend William E. Gardner—who was also a friend of the King family—determined Martin's "strongest points" to be his "clarity of expression, impressive personality," his chief weakness "an attitude of aloofness, disdain and possible snobbishness which prevent his coming to close grips with the rank and file of ordinary people. Also, a smugness that refuses to adapt itself to the demands of ministering effectively to the average Negro congregation."

The editors conclude from this that King had "become somewhat estranged from his Ebenezer roots." Other evidence suggests that he may have inherited the class consciousness that other family members had exhibited. The editors admit in the introduction that Martin's grandfather, A.D. Williams, had made money off a controversial business venture that targeted poor blacks. The black-run *Atlanta Independent* in 1909 called the stock that Williams was selling in a Mexican silver mine a "fake, pure and simple," and encouraged him "to explain . . . this fraudulent scheme" to the "many thousands of poor Negroes that are being defrauded throughout the state."

As Professor Enslin's letter to B.U. suggests, King was recommended for doctoral studies for reasons other than intellectual distinction and academic achievement. In fact, we know from his scores on the Graduate Record Exam that King scored in the second lowest quartile in English and vocabulary, in the lowest ten percent in quantitative analysis, and in the lowest third on his advanced test in philosophy—the very subject he would concentrate in at B.U. Instead, King was recommended because he socialized well with white students, had won white support and approval, could be of "useful service" in the future, and, so far from displaying any of those "annoying qualities" that other Negroes exhibited (whatever this means), had even showed a disdain toward Negroes of a lower socioeconomic order. It was clearly on the basis of race, not scholarship, that Enslin recommended King for doctoral studies.

The possibility that King benefited from an early form of affirmative action—from a lowering of academic standards or from preferential treatment because of his race—gains credence when his years of plagiarizing are considered. Though the editors treat this issue as gingerly as possible, their volume clearly proves that King was an inveterate plagiarist who began pilfering at an early age. The seminal speech he gave in Atlanta at the age of 15 is not only, as the editors say, "more polished than other pieces that King wrote as a teenager," it is more polished than anything King "wrote" as an adult in either college or seminary. The editors conclude that the "essay probably benefited from adult editing and from King's awareness of similar orations." Put more bluntly, the speech was either written by an adult or copped from an unknown source.

The evidence of King's pilferage is overwhelming. The editors do not highlight the stolen sections but simply reprint in footnotes without editorial comment the original passages King plagiarized, making the footnotes in this volume often as long and tedious as the documents themselves. Sample one of the many "borrowed" passages in King's essay on "Ritual," written as a junior or senior at Morehouse College:

King:	Plagiarized source:
All feasts are divided into two classes, feasts of precept and feasts of devotion. The feasts of precept are holydays [sic] on which the Faithful in most Catholic countries refrain from unnecessary servile labor and attend Mass. These include all the Sundays in the year, Christmas Day, the circumcism [sic] . . .	All feasts are divided into two classes, feasts of precept and feasts of devotion. The former are holy days on which the Faithful in most Catholic countries refrain from unnecessary servile labour and attend Mass. These include all the Sundays in the year, Christmas Day, the Circumcision . . .

From King's essay on "The Significant Contributions of Jeremiah to Religious Thought," written during his first term at Crozer:

King:
This Temple was the
pivot of the nation's religion. It was a national
institution, linked intimately with the fortunes of the
race. In the course of
years elaborate
ceremonies were
enacted, and the
priests prescribed sacrifices,
and the smoke of burnt-
offerings rose high from the
altar. The Temple was the
apple of the people's eye.
To criticise [*sic*] it was to set
aflame the fires of both religion and patriotism. And
this was the very thing
that Jeremiah did.

Plagiarized source:
[The Temple] was the . . .
pivot of the nation's religion. . . . It was a national
institution, linked intimately with the fortunes of the
race. . . . In the course of
centuries an elaborate litur-
gical ceremony came to be
enacted there, and the
priests prescribed sacrifices,
and the smoke of burnt-
offerings rose high from the
altar. . . . The Temple was the
apple of the people's eye.
To touch it was to set
aflame the fires of both religion and patriotism. And
this was just the very thing
that the prophet did.

King's plagiarisms are easy to detect because their style rises above the level of his pedestrian student prose. In general, if the sentences are eloquent, witty, insightful, or pithy, or contain allusions, analogies, metaphors, or similes, it is safe to assume that the section has been purloined. "To set aflame the fires of religion and patriotism," "It was the eye of Yahweh that was forever searching the thoughts and intents of the heart," "Evil is the Satan that laughs at logic," "Religion [is] the response of the heart to the voice of God"—all are flags of King's "textual appropriations."

In fact, King's plagiarisms grow more sweeping with each year he progresses in higher education. For instance, in his essay on "A Study of Mithraism," which he "composed" during his second year at Crozer, King lifts verbatim entire paragraphs from Franz Cumont's well-known *The Mysteries of Mithra* and W.R. Halliday's *The Pagan Background of Early Christianity*. Also evident in this essay is King's "composition method" of plagiarizing himself, meaning his recycling verbatim into "new" essays huge sections of compositions he had written in previous years for other classes.

But these examples from King's early terms at Crozer pale in comparison to the thefts committed during his final two years, and in particular to the papers King composed for Professor George Washington Davis. Carson and company see nothing unusual in the fact that King took *nine* courses from this professor, because "so theologically compatible were King and Davis" and because King "forged his own theological perspective" in Davis's courses, for which "King's essays . . . displayed a greater degree of intellectual engagement" than those he had written for other Crozer professors.

If what the editors say is true, King's compositions for Professor Davis should be the best argued, best written, most erudite and original of all his essays. The evidence suggests otherwise. From the introduction to King's "The Sources of Fundamentalism":

King:	*Plagiarized source:*
In the course of its develop- ment western civilization has shifted from a colonial naivete of the frontier to the far-reach- ing machination of national- ism and from an agrarian pattern of occupation to the industrial one....	In the course of its develop- ment western civilization has shifted from a colonial naivete of the frontier to the far-reach- ing machinations of national- ism and from an agrarian pattern of occupation to the industrial one....

Plagiarism continues throughout eight of the remaining 13 paragraphs of the essay.

From the introduction to King's "The Origin of Religion in the Race":

King:	*Plagiarized source:*
Before we come to consider some modern theories it may be well to refer briefly to two views which were once widely prevalent, but which	Before we come to consider some modern theories it may be well to refer briefly to two views which were once widely prevalent, but which

are now obsolete or	are now obsolete or
at least absolescent [*sic*].	obsolescent.

Only three of the remaining 22 paragraphs in the essay are not replete with verbatim plagiarisms, often of entire paragraphs.

From King's essay on "The Humanity and Divinity of Jesus":

King:	*Plagiarized sources:*
If there is any one thing of which modern Christians have been certain it is that Jesus was a true man, bone of our bone, flesh of our flesh, in all points tempted as we are. . . . Like the rest of us, he got hungry. When at the well of Sameria [*sic*] he asked the woman who was drawing water for a drink. When he grew tired, he needed rest and sleep. . . . On the Cross, he added to all physical tortures the final agony of feeling God-forsaken.	If there is any one thing of which Christians have been certain it is that Jesus is true man, bone of our bone, flesh of our flesh, in all points tempted as we are. . . . Like the rest of us, he was hungry. At the well at Samaria he asked the woman who was drawing water for a drink. When he grew tired, he needed rest and sleep. . . . On the Cross, he added to all physical tortures the final agony of feeling God-forsaken.

Regarding some of the other essays King wrote for Professor Davis, of the 37 paragraphs in his essay on "The Influence of the Mystery Religions on Christianity," 11 are recycled from two essays written in previous years and 24 of the remaining 26 paragraphs are replete with verbatim plagiarisms. In "The Origin of Religion in the Race," only four of the 24 paragraphs are free of verbatim theft. In "Religion's Answer to the Problem of Evil," only 14 of the 38 paragraphs are free of verbatim plagiarisms.

Again, Carson concludes from these "engaged" essays, which Davis routinely gave "A's," and from the nine courses King took from Davis, that the student and the professor were merely "compatible." A simpler conclusion is that the professor had been snowed.

We know from comments written on King's essays that some professors reprimanded him for incomplete footnotes, but there is no evidence to indicate that they ever realized the extent of King's pilfering.

The editors admit in their introduction that King's essays possess "unacknowledged textual appropriations," which "meet a strict definition of plagiarism," but they hasten to assure us that there is still no "definite answer to the question whether King deliberately violated the standards that applied to him as a student"! If the editors do not know what academic standards are, at least King himself did. He plainly states on page seven of his dissertation, "The present inquiry will utilize from these valuable secondary sources any results which bear directly on the problem, and will indicate such use by appropriate footnotes," and then proceeds to steal word-for-word and without any acknowledgment whatsoever huge sections from the thesis of Jack Boozer.

Eugene Genovese also admits King's pilferage, but writes off its significance as a mere "impatience with scholarly procedures," something that should not diminish our appreciation of King's "fine" mind. After all, King may have plagiarized his way through college, seminary, and graduate school, but this was "not an expression of laziness or an unwillingness to do the required work"! How can we ever know?

While Carson and his fellow apologists are making a heroic effort to palliate King's literary and academic shenanigans, Keith Miller boldly takes the bull by the horns. An assistant professor of English at Arizona State University, Miller cheerfully admits King's plagiarisms, or rather his "unattributed appropriations," "intertextualizations," "incorporations," "borrowings," "alchemizing," "overlapping," "adopting," "synthesizing," "replaying," "echoing," "resonances," "reverberations," and "voice merging." But far from wanting to trivialize the facts, Miller argues that King's pilferage was intentional, and even an integral and laudatory part of the civil rights movement. For by interweaving stolen texts into his speeches and essays, and by stealing in particular the words of liberal white ministers, King "foolproofed his discourse" and was able to "change the minds of moderate and uncommitted whites" toward solving "the nation's most horrific problem—racial injustice." This "method of composition" is what Miller terms "voice merging" and associates with the borrowing of sermons common among black folk preachers.

The most useful portions of this book are those in which Miller sets forth the sources of King's nonacademic works. He occasionally mentions King's famous antiwar speeches that were ghostwritten by Andrew Young and other supporters, but he highlights the pilfered sources behind King's landmark orations on civil rights. King's Nobel Prize Lecture, for example, is plagiarized extensively from works by Florida minister J. Wallace Hamilton; the sections on Gandhi and nonviolence in his "Pilgrimage" speech are stolen virtually verbatim from Harris Wofford's speech on the same topic; the frequently replayed climax to the "I Have a Dream" speech—the "from every mountainside, let freedom ring" portion—is taken directly from a 1952 address to the Republican National Convention by a black preacher named Archibald Carey; the 1968 sermon in which King prophesied his martyrdom was based on works by J. Wallace Hamilton and Methodist minister Harold Bosley; even the "Letter From Birmingham City Jail," that "great American essay" so often reproduced in textbooks on composition, is based on work by Harry Fosdick, H.H. Crane, and Harris Wofford—all sources King could recall from memory because of the frequency with which he had "merged" with them in the past.

Miller's research is indispensable for understanding King's works, but his intoxicating thesis proves fatal to his judgment:

> King's achievements are awesome. Borrowed sermons gave white Americans their best—and probably last—chance to solve what had always been the nation's worst problem. Not only did voice merging keep Jefferson's dream alive, it also helped compel the White House to withdraw from the nightmare of Vietnam. Then in the wake of his movement came the second wave of American feminism, the campaign for gay rights, and the crusade to save the environment.

All this owed to plagiarism! Miller apparently believes that every social and protest movement of our time is rooted in dishonesty.

A more fundamental problem with Miller's thesis is lack of proof. He offers no documentation, confession, or interview of any sort— nothing to prove that King deliberately plagiarized white sources to garner white support for the civil rights movement. Nor does his argument account for the plagiarisms King committed throughout college, seminary, and his doctoral studies—all of which occurred long before he ever became what Miller calls "the unofficial president of an oppressed people."

Miller explains away such pilferage with his "voice merging" theory—that King plagiarized because he was unable (and still unable after 11 years of higher education and three academic degrees) to separate himself from the black homiletic tradition of "borrowing" other people's work. On one level, this argument is equivalent to saying "King's plagiarism is a black thing. You whites with your standards wouldn't understand." But the deeper implication is that originality and true scholarship cannot be expected of blacks, that because of their oral traditions blacks cannot differentiate between the pulpit and the classroom, between Sunday sermons and professional standards, between the mores of folk art and the demands of high culture. How flattering this is to all the black doctors, black lawyers, black theologians, and black scholars who have made and continue to make their way honestly in the world.

Miller concludes by suggesting that the country should be grateful for King's commitment to plagiarism. For stealing the works of others "let King escape the restrictions of the clock and therein become a Houdini of time. . . . This ubiquitous leader could magically advise senators, write a column, publish an essay, rally voters, placate unruly staffers, preach a sermon, and comfort a church janitor—all in a single day. . . . Barnstorming the nation as a Houdini of time became possible only because King consulted sources and thereby foolproofed his discourse." King was indeed a master of illusion and deception, but his discourse was hardly foolproof.

ELEVEN

Letter from Peter Wood of Boston University to *Chronicles*

Assistant Provost Peter Wood of Boston University sent the following response to the review essay reprinted in the previous chapter. It appeared in the March 1993 issue of Chronicles.

In his review of the first volume of *The Papers of Martin Luther King, Jr.* (Opinions, November 1992), Theodore Pappas errs in asserting that Boston University was part of the effort to "whitewash" the plagiarism in King's Ph.D. dissertation. Mr. Jon Westling, who was then president ad interim of the university, was among those who took the King papers' editor, Dr. Clayborne Carson, at his word when he said he and his colleagues had found no evidence of plagiarism in the dissertation.

The rumor that Dr. King plagiarized some unspecified part of his dissertation first reached the university in May 1990, when Professor John Shelton Reed sent the university a copy of what purported to be a forthcoming article in *Chronicles*. Even though the article offered no specifics, Jon Westling responded immediately by asking me to call Clayborne Carson. I did and reported Dr. Carson's unequivocal assurances that the rumor had no foundation in fact. Mr. Westling nonetheless followed up by contacting all the living members of Dr. King's dissertation committee, as well as other members of the faculty who taught Dr. King when he was a student at Boston University (1951-1955), and asking them if they had any idea what lay behind the rumor. Finally, he began the laborious process of reviewing the dissertation to search for instances of plagiarism from an unknown source.

The short-term result of these efforts is that we found nothing to contradict Dr. Carson's claims. Mr. Westling subsequently wrote back to Professor Reed and said that if he had specific evidence, he should reveal it, and if he didn't have evidence, he should refrain from making such serious allegations. Reed replied that he was withdrawing the article.

Four months later, with no further notice and without citing any evidence, *Chronicles* printed the still unsubstantiated rumor that Dr. King's dissertation was plagiarized. Mr. Westling subsequently wrote to your magazine with the facts as they then appeared. His letter explicitly said that "if you or anyone has evidence . . . it should be presented." Mr. Pappas now quotes that letter out of context to make it appear that Mr. Westling was among those willing to bend the truth to protect Dr. King's reputation. Mr. Pappas is fully aware of the actual sequence of events. His deliberate distortion of the record in this instance (and how many others?) taints his demand for a more forthright accounting of Dr. King's career as a plagiarist. His review is a reminder that there is more than one way to be intellectually dishonest.

TWELVE

Editorial response to Mr. Wood
by Theodore Pappas

The following response to Mr. Wood appeared in the March 1993 issue of Chronicles.

Boston University has apparently learned nothing from its embarrassing correspondence of two years ago—when it sent for publication in the January 1991 *Chronicles* a letter claiming "not a single reader has ever found any nonattributed or misattributed quotations, misleading paraphrases, or thoughts borrowed without due scholarly reference in any of its [King's thesis] 343 pages."

I closed my January 1991 article with some simple logic, that no matter how this matter played out, B.U.'s reputation had been seriously damaged. B.U. officials either knew about King's pilfering and deliberately withheld the evidence or were incapable of detecting the plagiarisms in the first place and remained too incompetent to find them now. These were and still are the only two possible conclusions.

Thanks to Mr. Wood, we now know it was the latter. Apparently Jon Westling wasn't lying—he truly was incapable of finding the plagiarisms, even after "the laborious process of reviewing the dissertation," which produced "nothing to contradict Dr. Carson's claims." Mr. Wood apparently believes that he does his university credit by highlighting the ineptitude of its administration. How reassuring this defense must be to B.U. students and their parents, alumni and faculty.

Mr. Wood calls the job of detecting King's plagiarisms "laborious."

To set the record straight, the task is nothing of the sort; the plagiarisms are so blatant that their detection is easy.

Rumors of King's plagiarisms and even of his prime source, Jack Boozer, had circulated in scholarly circles for many years. The London *Telegraph* had written about them two years earlier, in 1989. But even if Jon Westling didn't know about Boozer's thesis before he began his "laborious" investigation, one of King's principal sources for his dissertation is nevertheless easy to ascertain. King acknowledges in his introduction, on pages five and seven, that three years earlier at B.U. Boozer had written a "fine" thesis on the *same* subject of Paul Tillich and that he would cite it appropriately whenever he drew upon it. Even the most cursory perusal of King's footnotes is sufficient to see that King scarcely mentions Boozer at all.

Mr. Wood also denies that B.U. attempted to whitewash this issue. On the committee that B.U. president John Silber convened to analyze King's and Boozer's theses sat the university's "Martin Luther King Professor of Social Ethics," John Cartwright. After months on the committee supposedly analyzing the dissertations, and long after even Clayborne Carson had given up the charade and admitted that King's thesis was replete with "textual appropriations," B.U.'s professor of "social ethics" still publicly claimed that "there is no obvious indication in the dissertation that he [King] inappropriately utilized material." A better example of whitewashing could hardly be found.

It was B.U.'s reputation, not Mr. King's, that was riding on the committee's handling of this controversy. We all know what King did; the only question was whether B.U. as an institution devoted to the pursuit of truth would have the honesty and integrity to admit its mistakes and acknowledge King's wrongdoings. Mr. Wood tells us the answer is no.

THIRTEEN

"Truth or Consequences: Redefining Plagiarism" by Theodore Pappas

The following essay appeared in the September 1993 issue of Chronicles.

A Trojan horse has passed through the gates of the academy, virtually unnoticed. The Sinon is Keith Miller, an assistant professor of English at Arizona State University and author of *Voice of Deliverance: The Language of Martin Luther King, Jr., and Its Sources* (1992), and the subversive offering is his essay in the January 20 issue of the *Chronicle of Higher Education*: "Redefining Plagiarism: Martin Luther King's Use of an Oral Tradition."

Considering the cowardliness and disingenuousness with which the scholarly community has greeted the revelations of King's literary thefts, this call for a kinder and gentler definition of plagiarism in light of King's chicanery is not surprising. Miller argues that King's plagiarisms should not be condemned but rather "understood" in context of the "black experience." Because King was black as well as a preacher, and because black preachers traditionally "voice merge" with one another by freely borrowing sermons without attribution, Miller concludes that King's plagiarisms must have derived from his inability to separate himself from this homiletic tradition and to comprehend the standards of an alien "white" culture—this even after 11 years of higher education, three academic degrees, and a Boston University seminar on plagiarism and scholarly standards.

Since many minorities come from cultures rich in oral traditions,

Miller urges the academy to redefine plagiarism to accommodate these "excluded" groups. To put this more bluntly, all legal claims to original thought and the interpretation of ideas must now be nullified in deference to multiculturalism, cultural relativism, and universal human rights. Like the long list of taboos to have fallen before it, plagiarism must now be updated and redefined in accordance with social progress. For "the process of securing fundamental human rights," argues Miller, "such as those King championed—outweighs the right to the exclusive use of intellectual and literary property."

To Miller's chagrin, what's good for the goose is apparently not also good for the gander. As copyright expert Robert Cassler points out in the February 24 issue of the *Chronicle of Higher Education*, "Dr. King vigorously defended his copyright in 'I Have a Dream' when others wanted to use it. (See *King* v. *Mister Maestro, Inc.* . . . 1963)." This is doubly interesting when one recalls that King plagiarized the famous climax to the "I Have a Dream" speech from a 1952 address to the Republican National Convention by a little-known black preacher named Archibald Carey.

Miller is proud of where this revolution in standards will lead. "A lawyer asked me for advice in defending a Native American student charged with plagiarizing papers in law school," he states. "The student came from an oral culture, and could not immediately understand or obey the rules of written English. . . . King's example thus is not an isolated case." Indeed, Miller's call for a new conception of plagiarism should have little trouble gaining the support of both the ABA and the U.S. Student Association, as "voice merging" is a godsend to lawyer and plagiarist alike.

Miller's defense of King and his novel approach to plagiarism are both predictable. Polygamy, female circumcision, animal sacrifices, and witchcraft have all become acceptable so long as they are practices of preferred minorities, and if Mr. King seduced underage girls, then statutory rape must be redefined as mere erotic exuberance or as an assault on children's rights. Miller's sophistry and skewed logic produce just such absurdities. "Simply put," he writes, "we face a contradiction: We wish to lionize a man for his powerful language while decrying a major strategy that made his words resonate and persuade." Then for the howling non sequitur: "How could such a compelling leader commit what most people define as a writer's worst sin? The contradiction should prompt us to rethink our definition of plagiarism." And we should rethink drunk driving in light of Chappaquiddick and redefine adultery to accommodate King's philandering.

In better days the follies of our heroes did not move us to subvert the moral underpinnings of our culture. Great falls were lamented but expected of Fallen Man; they were the unavoidable acts in the tragedy of life, and the lessons they taught formed the grist of our greatest literature. But a rhetoric of accountability has little appeal today and pales before the lure of "diseases," "addictions," and novel theories of human behavior that conveniently exonerate us from responsibility for our actions. Marion Barry, when caught cavorting with drug dealers and smoking crack cocaine while mayor of D.C., didn't let down his constituency, make a mockery of political office, shirk his responsibilities, break laws, to say nothing of trivializing the real problems plaguing the black community. No, he simply had an addiction and needed a couple of months of counseling to build his self-esteem. Baseball star Wade Boggs, who blubbered on national television that he was "addicted to sex," didn't lie to his wife, neglect his children, and cheat his teammates and his fans by playing ball only halfheartedly when his wife rather than his mistress was watching from the stands; his "disease" did. And similarly with King. He didn't take the words of others, claim them as his own, and then go to court to protect his purloined property. No, he simply acted within a rich but little appreciated tradition to which the majority culture must learn to be sensitive.

Miller, it should be noted, is white, which is not an inconsequential fact. For it is whites who have led the fight to palliate King's plagiarisms and who have given new meaning to the term "whitewash." It is the moguls of the majority culture in both the academy and the press who continue to praise Clayborne Carson of the King Papers Project for his "honesty" and "integrity," even though Carson learned about King's thefts in 1987 and admittedly lied about the evidence (while accepting public funds as an editor) for three years thereafter. Miller, in his book, even floats the absurdity that plagiarizing was perhaps King's greatest gift to the country, for without stealing the words of white scholars and preachers for his articles and speeches, King could never have sold whites on the civil rights movement.

Jon Westling, John Silber, and Peter Wood of Boston University, as well as all but one member of the committee that B.U. convened to examine King's thesis, are also white. As the committee concluded in its September 1991 report, because King plagiarized only 45 percent of the first half of his dissertation and only 21 percent of the second, the thesis remains a legitimate and "intelligent contribution to scholarship" about which "no thought should be given to the revocation of Dr. King's doctoral degree." Funny, B.U. would give "no thought" to revoking King's fraudulently earned doctorate, but when its own dean of the Boston University College of Communication, H. Joachim Maitre, stole numerous paragraphs from an essay by film critic Michael Medved for his May 1991 commencement address—a mere case of "voice merging"—it demoted him to the ranks. S. Paul Schilling, who was the second reader of King's dissertation, states in a letter B.U. reproduces in its report that "it should be recognized that [King's] appropriation of the language of others does not entail inaccurate interpretation of the thought of writers cited"—as if King deserves praise for stealing accurately—and notes that King was "operating on a very crowded schedule during most of the work on his dissertation"—as if theft is excusable if one is busy and in a hurry.

These embarrassing exonerations and rationalizations of King's plagiarisms are more damaging to blacks than if B.U. had revoked King's doctorate. For by excusing King's pilferings—and in Miller's case, by excusing them as "a black thing"—King's apologists are telling black scholars everywhere that they shouldn't bother doing their own work, or worse, that no black can really pull his own weight, write his own papers, or actually become a professional like white people can. When Miller argues that the accomplishments of blacks should be held to different and clearly less-demanding standards, that they should be discounted in light of the "black oral tradition," he takes a backhand to every black scholar honestly pursuing his craft.

Put simply, these specious attempts to exonerate King are primarily "a white thing," not a black. This is hardly surprising. They appear, in fact, strikingly similar to many other acts of penitence—such as affirmative action, quotas, and the race-norming of government exams—that a guilt-ridden white community has felt duty-bound to perform in expiation of racial sins, both real and imagined. But if they waft of something new, of something characteristic of our more "sensitive" and enlightened present, they just as surely smack of something very old, something redolent of the very age we have tried to exorcise and discredit. For these spurious rationalizations of King's wrongdoings are nothing if not also a manifestation of what Kipling termed the "white man's burden," of that pernicious form of paternalism that breeds lies and deceptions and that oppresses the very people intended to be uplifted.

This whitewash of King's actions has many antecedents. It was the white media that appointed Jesse Jackson over Ralph Abernathy to succeed King at the head of the civil rights movement. They were the ones who publicized Jackson's lies about cradling the dying King, who published the photographs of the bogus bloody shirt, and who since then have buried all mention of this particular act of crass opportunism for which King's closest followers never forgave Jackson. Philip Nobile, whose exposé in the February 23 issue of the *Village Voice* revealed the extent to which Alex Haley plagiarized and fabricated his "autobiography" *Roots*, reminds us that it was an all-white, 17-man jury that awarded Haley the Pulitzer Prize for his stolen work of fiction. (Haley paid a $650,000 settlement in an unpublicized plagiarism suit shortly before he died.) "If we blew the Haley prize, as we apparently did, I feel bad," William McGill—former president of Columbia University and an *ex officio* presence on the 1977 Pulitzer Prize board—told Nobile. "The answer to that question [whether race affected the board's decision] is yes. . . . We all labored under the delusion that sudden expressions of love could make up for historical mistakes. . . . Of course, that's inverse racism."

Hustlers and hucksters like Malcolm X—"hustler" being Malcolm's description of himself in his "autobiography," written by Alex Haley—and the Reverend Al Sharpton, who still claims Tawana Brawley was molested by white racists, are also largely the creation of the white media. As is the infamous film on World War II by Nina Rosenblum and William Miles called *The Liberators*, which purports that the "true" liberator of Hitler's most notorious concentration camps was an all-black unit of the U.S. Army. PBS televised the film nationally and hailed it as an invaluable look at a shamefully neglected aspect of world history; Hollywood plugged it as the "best documentary of the year" and quickly nominated it for an Academy Award; and yet the film has been quietly pulled from circulation, as even black veterans from the very unit supposedly responsible for the liberations have denounced it as balderdash and blatant propaganda.

Nietzsche believed "one may sometimes tell a lie, but the grimace with which one accompanies it tells the truth." If our culture's infatuation with lies is any indication, Nietzsche clearly underestimated the modern mastery of the straight face.

ABOUT THE EDITOR . . .

Theodore Pappas is the managing editor of *Chronicles: A Magazine of American Culture*, a publication of The Rockford Institute in Rockford, Illinois. He was educated at Beloit College and Harvard University, where he studied American intellectual history. His writings have appeared in such journals as the *American Scholar*, *Modern Age*, *Human Events*, *Humanitas*, *This World*, and the *Wilson Quarterly*, as well as numerous newspapers nationwide. He received the Hessletine Award for historical writing in 1988.